the **DAY** of the

PREPARING TO MEET THE BRIDEGROOM

LORD

by Bill Mills

FOREWORD BY REV. PATRICK PEGLOW

BOOKS BY LEADERSHIP RESOURCES

Connecting With One Another Series

These devotional Bible studies are designed for personal growth as well as classes and small groups. Each book contains a 9-week discussion guide.

The Path of Joy: Enjoying Intimacy with God
by Marnie Carlson

Friendly Fire: Why Is God Shooting at Me?
by William G. Johnson

Changed: Experiencing God's Transforming Power
(Also available in Chinese)
by Bill Mills

Naked & Unashamed: Recapturing Family Intimacy
(Also available in Spanish and Chinese)
by Bill Mills

A Quiet Heart: Discovering Peace & Power at Jesus' Feet
by Carla Jividen Peer

Beyond Independence: Reclaiming Our Life Together in Christ
by Bill Mills

Pursuing God: Finding Our Fullness in Christ
(Also available in Chinese)
by Bill Mills

Shoulder to Shoulder: How God Builds Spiritual Men
(Also available in Chinese)
by Bill Mills

The Day of the Lord! Preparing to Meet the Bridegroom
by Bill Mills

The Blessing of Benjamin:
Living in the Power of Your Father's Approval
by Bill Mills and Peter Luisi-Mills

Connecting With God for Growth and Ministries Series

These devotional Bible studies will help you grow in your relationship with the Lord and in your ministry.

Adequate! How God Empowers Ordinary People to Serve
(Also available in Chinese)
by Bill Mills

Language of the Heart: Knowing Joy and Communion in Prayer
by Bill Mills

Finishing Well in Life and Ministry:
God's Protection from Burnout
(Also available in Spanish and Chinese)
by Bill Mills and Craig Parro

Unlikely Warriors: Our Call to Invade the Darkness
by Craig Parro

Inductive Bible Study Series

These Bible study helps will enable you to grow in your understanding of the Scriptures and in your preparation for teaching.

Proverbs: Lessons for the Growing Years (for Jr/Sr High)

Jonah: Inductive Bible Study

Philippians: A Family Bible Study

Ruth: The Romance of Redemption

Inductive Bible Study Handbook
by Dennis Fledderjohann

A Servant Series

Each book contains 21 articles from many well-known authors. Great library resources!

Marriage, Parenting & Forgiveness

Reconciliation, Fellowship & the Grace of God

You may order our books and Bible conference CDs on our web site:
www.LeadershipResources.org

Fourth Printing—2007

THIS MINISTRY IS DEDICATED TO

The Glory of God
The Honor of His Word
The Building Up of the Body of Christ

Since all these things are thus to be dissolved, what sort of people ought you to be in lives of holiness and godliness,

2 Peter 3:11

Table of Contents

Foreword *by*

Rev. Patrick Peglow

Senior Pastor, Moraine Valley Church
Palos Heights, IL

During my years of school, I learned many valuable truths about God, the Bible, ministry and walking with God. But I was reminded in school that "some things are better caught than taught." The very first day that I officially entered full-time pastoral ministry, God gave me a gift by bringing another man on the staff as a fellow pastor, a man whom I had only met briefly on one other occasion. That man was Bill Mills. Bill had already been in the ministry for years and he, along with my senior pastor at that time, Bill Johnson, were the two men that God used in my life to enable me to see what ministry and walking with God looks like. From these two men I have caught more about ministry and walking with God than I did in 8 years of Bible college and seminary. Over these last 18 years, Bill and I have formed a friendship

9

that we share with one another on a very personal level. Now as a senior pastor, I often look to Bill as someone who is further down the road, for the counsel I need as a man, a pastor, a preacher and a leader. Bill has truly been one of God's great gifts to me and to our church over the years.

This book, *The Day of the Lord*, is another precious gift that God has given to his people. We are living in a time when many world events seem to indicate that the stage is being set for the return of the Lord for His Bride, the Church. Along with these momentous times has come a heightened interest in prophecy. Most current books and conferences on prophecy draw from Scripture very valuable details about prophecy and then relate current events from our world to them. This book has a different focus as it encourages us from Scripture as to what kind of lives we ought to live in light of the return of the Lord. In *The Day of the Lord*, Bill moves beyond the "what" of prophecy to the "why" God revealed these truths to us. He moves us from the classroom of prophecy into an everyday life that is to be shaped by the ultimate implications of these prophecies. This book serves as a bridge between the ever-increasing gulf between the "theology" of prophecy and the "transformation" that prophecy is to produce.

The Day of the Lord explores the many different implications of the very sobering statement that Peter made nearly 2000 years ago, a statement that still has deep implications upon our lives today, every day, all day long.

> But the day of the Lord will come like a thief, and then the heavens will pass away with a roar, and the heavenly bodies will be burned up and dissolved, and the earth and the works that are done on it will be exposed. Since all these things are thus to be dissolved, what sort of people ought you to be in lives of holiness and godliness, waiting for and hastening the coming of the day of God, because of which the heavens will be set on fire and dis-

solved, and the heavenly bodies will melt as they burn! But according to his promise we are waiting for new heavens and a new earth in which righteousness dwells. (2 Peter 3:10-13)

My prayer is that God will use this book to make us a people whose lives in this present world will be transformed by the hope of the yet future *Day of the Lord*.

This is now the second letter that I am writing to you, be-loved. In both of them I am stirring up your sincere mind by way of reminder,

2 Peter 3:1

Introduction

How valuable it is to be reminded of those things that are most important to us as the children of God! In the battles of life and the demands of our relationships and responsibilities, we tend to lose our focus. The Apostle Peter loved to remind God's people what was most important in the midst of their urgent and demanding circumstances. His second letter is filled with reminders for us. It also culminates in calling us to focus again on the highest priority of our lives: preparing to meet our Lord when He returns.

The Apostle Peter had a heart to call God's people back to the most significant aspects of our lives. In chapter one of his letter, after describing the progressive walk of faith and obedience in which we become fruitful in the Kingdom of God, he said:

> Therefore I intend always to remind you of these qualities, though you know them and are established in the truth that you have. (2 Peter 1:12)

Even after we have a deep understanding of the truth and are firmly established in it, we still need to be reminded of what we possess in Christ. A knowledge of the truth alone, as foundational and critical as that is, is not sufficient to carry us to godliness and fruitfulness in life, relationships and ministry. We need to live today in the freshness and the power of who we are in Christ and with all of the Holy Spirit's resources enabling us to experience the life the Father has given us in His Son:

> I think it right, as long as I am in this body, to stir you up by way of reminder, since I know that the putting off of my body will be soon, as our Lord Jesus Christ made clear to me. (2 Peter 1:13-14)

"LET ME REMIND YOU"

Peter made it his lifelong ministry to remind the churches of those things at the center of God's heart and purposes. We, too, need to be reminded because it is the nature of our flesh to forget so quickly the priorities of our Father for us. Peter's purpose is my purpose as I share this study with you. Too often we become convinced that some exciting new truth, one that no one else has ever discovered or explained this way before, will be the "key" to transforming our lives, our families, our churches and our ministries. But what we need most is to be reminded of the historical teachings of the Scriptures and the bedrock realities of God's revelation to us in Christ.

As Peter began chapter three of his second letter, he told us that both of his letters had the very same purpose:

> This is now the second letter that I am writing to you, beloved. In both of them I am stirring up your sincere mind by way of reminder, (2 Peter 3:1)

Peter's desire is to stimulate our "sincere mind." The Apostle encourages us to sincere thinking that flows from a pure heart. The truth is, we lose our perspective so easily. We are bombarded with the mindset of this world, and in the relentless battles of life and the flesh, we tend to lose our bearings. We need to be brought back into a proper view of God, of ourselves and of His purposes. Wholesome thinking is a life perspective grounded deeply in the thoughts of our eternal God.

How do we arrive at this kind of thinking; how do we gain God's perspective again? Through a fuller understanding of the Word of God! Peter calls us to remember the teaching of the prophets and that of the Lord Jesus by His apostles:

> that you should remember the predictions of the holy prophets and the commandment of the Lord and Savior through your apostles, (2 Peter 3:2)

THE WORD OF GOD BRINGS WHOLESOME THINKING

The Scriptures bring to us the mind of God. They alone give us the perspective of our heavenly Father and enable us to look at life through His eyes. The whole of the Word of God brings us His thoughts, His ways and His world view. Many years before the Lord Jesus appeared and Peter wrote his letter, the prophet Isaiah wrote these words:

> For my thoughts are not your thoughts, neither are your ways my ways, declares the LORD. For as the heavens are higher than the earth, so are my ways higher than your ways and my thoughts than your thoughts. (Isaiah 55:8-9)

A finite mind cannot comprehend the perspectives of an infinite God. His thoughts are in a completely different realm, from a kingdom beyond the grasp of our minds. Only as God opens Himself to be known to us and reveals His thoughts and His ways can we see and understand. This happens through the ministry of His Word and His Spirit:

> For as the rain and the snow come down from heaven and do not return there but water the earth, making it bring forth and sprout, giving seed to the sower and bread to the eater, so shall my word be that goes out from my mouth; it shall not return to me empty, but it shall accomplish that which I purpose, and shall succeed in the thing for which I sent it. (Isaiah 55:10-11)

The Word that has gone out from the mouth of our glorious and faithful God has come through the prophets and the apostles. The prophets spoke of God's purposes from the beginning, and the apostles brought forth the commands of the Lord Jesus. In fact, as Peter says "your apostles," he is bringing that sense of authority found in his apostleship. The words that he is writing in this letter are the words of God. They are coming forth from His mouth.

That means that these words that Peter wrote in his second letter should have authority in our lives as well. The way we view our lives and orient our priorities will not only be guided but also transformed by what we read in these Scriptures. Peter is calling us to faith, to obedience and endurance, to missions and evangelism. He is challenging us to demonstrate holiness, to guard our lives and to prepare for The Day of the Lord!

The title for our book comes from this same chapter, 2 Peter 3, which is the basis for this Bible study:

> But the day of the Lord will come like a thief, and then the heavens will pass away with a roar, and the heavenly bodies will be burned up and dissolved, and the earth and the works that are done on it will be exposed. (2 Peter 3:10)

THE DAY OF THE LORD

As the prophets of old talked of "The Day of the Lord," it was with a sense of judgment, but also with a deep and genuine hope. Malachi described it in this way:

Behold, I will send you Elijah the prophet before the great and awesome day of the LORD comes. (Malachi 4:5)

Malachi talks of the day of the Lord as "great and dreadful." Jesus tells us in Matthew 11:7-15 that this prophecy concerning Elijah was fulfilled in John the Baptist. But notice also the sense of hope that Malachi brings:

And he will turn the hearts of fathers to their children and the hearts of children to their fathers, lest I come and strike the land with a decree of utter destruction. (Malachi 4:6)

We see the same sense in Joel's prophecy. As we contemplate his description of The Day of the Lord, our hearts are gripped with fear:

The sun shall be turned to darkness, and the moon to blood, before the great and awesome day of the LORD comes. (Joel 2:31)

If the sun is darkened and the moon turns to blood, how can we continue to exist? Changes like this would mean the end of all things that make our physical lives possible. Look with me, however, at the context of Joel's prophecy:

And it shall come to pass afterward, that I will pour out my Spirit on all flesh; your sons and your daughters shall prophesy, your old men shall dream dreams, and your young men shall see visions. Even on the male and female servants in those days I will pour out my Spirit. And I will show wonders in the heavens and on the earth, blood and fire and columns of smoke. (Joel 2:28-30)

Joel prefaces his statement on The Day of the Lord with his prophecy of God sending His Holy Spirit and pouring Him out on all mankind. And then, after his comment on The Day of the Lord, he sets before us this wonderful truth:

> And it shall come to pass that everyone who calls on the name of the LORD shall be saved. For in Mount Zion and in Jerusalem there shall be those who escape, as the LORD has said, and among the survivors shall be those whom the LORD calls. (Joel 2:32)

This promise is for you and me, for our loved ones and the nations: whoever calls on the name of the Lord will be saved. The Apostle Paul quotes from Joel's prophecy as he teaches on God's heart for salvation in his letter to the Romans:

> For there is no distinction between Jew and Greek; the same Lord is Lord of all, bestowing his riches on all who call on him. For "everyone who calls on the name of the Lord will be saved." (Romans 10:12-13)

For those of us who have placed our faith in Christ, The Day of the Lord will be one of salvation, hope and joy. For those who refuse to believe, The Day of the Lord will be a day of dread, fear and destruction.

THE LONG RANGE VIEW OF THE PROPHETS

We have seen that when the Old Testament prophets spoke of The Day of the Lord, they combined God's revelation of judgment to come with the hope of redemption and salvation. They were not able to discern clearly that these two prophetic perspectives would be fulfilled in two separate comings of Jesus, the Son of God. He would be born in a stable in Bethlehem when He came as the Lamb of God to take away our sins, dying on Calvary's cross as the Redeemer for all who would believe. But His revelation before the world as the Lion of Judah to judge the heavens and the earth—and to reign in the fullness of His power, holiness and glory—would be fulfilled in His Second Coming.

The view of the Old Testament prophets is something like the view we obtain by driving from the Midwest of the United States westward to the Rocky Mountains. Climbing upward through the Great Plains, from hundreds of miles away, one begins to see mountain peaks. In some places what we see are only a few very large and tall mountains. We cannot see the ranges with the many peaks and valleys in between. We are taking a long distance view into what lies ahead. That is the way it was for the prophets. They were looking ahead as God was revealing His plans for the future to them, but they could not see that the prophecies for His Messiah to be revealed as the Lamb and the Lion would be fulfilled in two separate appearances.

The Day of the Lord begins with the resurrection of the redeemed and Christ's Church meeting Him in the air, and culminates in His Second Coming to judge the world and to establish the new heaven and the new earth. I will tell you now that I am not a strong student of eschatology or "end time events." My heart and ministry are focused on encouraging churches and missions to walk in holiness and obedience before the Lord and to live as servants of one another. Yet, I know that studying the fulfillment of prophetic teachings is foundational to holy living. This understanding has drawn my heart to Peter's teaching in the third chapter of his second letter.

HEART PRIORITIES LOST IN THE DETAILS

I have been concerned about the way we as a Church today often get caught up in the myriad of prophetic details at the expense of higher priorities. This came home to me in a new way just a few months ago as I was returning home to Chicago from a time of teaching in the Los Angeles area. One of my greatest joys in life is seeing my wife Karen waiting for me at the airport when I arrive.

But on the flight home, I was thinking how different my return might be if Karen handled my trip the way we often deal with prophecy.

When I walked off the plane, I did not see Karen. I quickly looked around, and then I saw her running down the concourse toward me. I threw my arms around her and kissed her, but she was most anxious to tell me some things that had excited her. "I'm sorry I was almost late," she said, "but I was so fascinated studying about your trip. Did you know that you had a choice of four different airports for your flight to Chicago and that you could have flown on any one of eight airlines?" I told her that I really hadn't given it much thought. "I was on the Internet and I couldn't believe the amount of information available. It was so interesting! Did you know that your flight was exactly 1745 miles?" I really wanted to ask about her day, but Karen just went on. She said, "Normally, your flight United #114 takes about four hours, but today you had a tailwind of 89 miles per hour, and so your flight took only three hours and nineteen minutes! You were flying on a Boeing 757 which is the most fuel efficient airplane flying today." I was looking for an opening to ask how she was doing, but there wasn't room for even one word.

"A 757 holds 182 passengers, 24 in first class. Your plane had 162 people. This plane has two Pratt & Whitney engines, each producing 36,600 pounds of thrust! It is one of the safest airplanes flying. Its wingspan is 124 feet 10 inches, its length is 155 feet 3 inches, and the height of its tail is 44 feet 6 inches! In addition to the passengers, your plane was carrying 24,000 pounds of cargo." I had hoped to tell her about the days of ministry, but Karen was on a roll!

"Did you know that your plane was carrying 11,276 pounds of fuel? It weighed 255,000 pounds at takeoff. You were cruising at 35,600 feet, and..." Karen obviously had a further wealth of information to share with me, but I was finally able to get her attention to let me say a word. "All of that is really important, honey, but what I really wanted was for you to be here, ready when I arrived. I was hoping that you were longing to see my face!"

Karen had the most quizzical expression on her face. She looked at me and just said, "Oh."

Of course, that didn't happen because Karen is always excited about my homecoming. Her heart and her life are also centered on Christ's return and becoming the person He has called her to be. She has given herself to serve me and our sons, the ministry we share and the Church of the Lord Jesus Christ.

We thank God for every student of prophecy and every teacher that has helped us understand the meaning of the Scriptures that point to Christ's imminent return. All of these things are foundationally important. But let us never forget that the heart of prophetic teaching is focused on preparing us to meet the Bridegroom!

Warren Wiersbe talked of our vulnerability in the study of prophetic teaching in this way:

> The purpose of prophetic truth is not speculation but motivation; thus Peter concluded his letter with the kind of practical admonitions that all of us must heed. It is unfortunate when people run from one prophetic conference to another, filling their notebooks, marking their Bibles, drawing their charts, and yet not living their lives to the glory of God. In fact, some of the saints battle each other more over prophetic interpretation than perhaps any other subject.[1]

---

[1] Warren W. Wiersbe, *The Bible Exposition Commentary* (Wheaton, IL: Victor Books, 1989), p. 466.

21

The Day of the Lord!

That will be the focus of our study of 2 Peter 3. As we look at The Day of the Lord, we will not deal with many details of prophesy. We will look instead at Peter's encouragements to prepare our hearts. May God keep our hearts focused on the Bridegroom! It is our prayer that this study will be part of our Father's process to prepare us personally and as a Church for our Lord's return.

IT IS *HIS* DAY!

The most important thing for us to know about The Day of the Lord is that it is *His Day*. It is God's day to reign in righteousness, to display His glory, to judge wickedness, to pour out His wrath upon His enemies and to bring His Bride home to Himself. It is His day to finalize every design for time in His Son, and to fulfill every purpose for history.

When Jesus was arrested in the garden, He said to the chief priests, the temple guards and the elders who had come for Him:

> When I was with you day after day in the temple, you did not lay hands on me. But this is your hour, and the power of darkness. (Luke 22:53)

There is a day when God allows darkness to reign. It is seen in the fall of mankind; it is seen in the crucifixion of the Lord of glory; it is seen in the holocausts of history that have flowed from the hatred of our hearts. Even in that day, God is sovereign and is seated on His throne. In the midst of the evil, He is building the Church of His Son and a Kingdom that will never pass away. But there is another Day coming. It will be glorious and triumphant. On that Day, God will be revealed, time will be fulfilled, and we will reign with Him.

That is the Day for which Peter is calling us to prepare. May we follow his encouragements with whole hearts. When our Lord returns, may we be found seeking holiness, aggressively advancing in missions, enduring in our faith and longing to see our Lover's face!

They will say, "Where is the promise of his coming? For ever since the fathers fell asleep, all things are continuing as they were from the beginning of creation."

2 Peter 3:4

1

Where Is This Coming He Promised?

As I begin writing this chapter, I am in Brisbane, Australia, teaching at a wonderful church named Redcliffe Christian Assembly. I have taught here on several occasions, and it is good to be back with so many good friends. The message I gave this morning was the first session of our Bible conference, and I am excited about what God will do today by His Word and His Spirit.

After preaching the morning message, a young man began to visit with me. He told me of a cousin who no longer believed in God and wondered how to pray for him. It seems that their grandfather was a pastor, and one of his favorite themes was preaching on the Second Coming of Christ. "The Lord may return today," the preacher would often challenge his family and his congregation. "Well, that was three generations ago," this young man said, "and nothing has changed." Jesus still had not returned, and his cousin had concluded that waiting and living for His return was a waste of time. Now this young person is living for himself rather than for the Lord.

That thinking is not at all uncommon today; in fact, it is the predominant mindset of many Christians. It is also the prevailing perspective of many that attend our churches every week. The call to live and work for Christ and to prepare our hearts for His return has become so familiar to us that it has seemingly lost its power to move us to obedience and holiness. So many of our people have also concluded that if it has been so many generations since Jesus promised to come back, it is almost pointless to really believe that He may, in fact, return today.

JESUS PROMISED TO RETURN TO EARTH

The Apostle Peter was one of the eyewitnesses when Christ, after appearing before his disciples for forty days, gave His disciples this command:

> And while staying with them he ordered them not to depart from Jerusalem, but to wait for the promise of the Father, which, he said, "you heard from me; for John baptized with water, but you will be baptized with the Holy Spirit not many days from now." (Acts 1:4-5)

This promise was fulfilled in the day of Pentecost, about ten days later, when the Holy Spirit came with great power upon the one hundred twenty believers gathered in the upper room. On that day the Church of the Lord Jesus was born. But the disciples were still confused and most concerned about the kingdom of this world:

> So when they had come together, they asked him, "Lord, will you at this time restore the kingdom to Israel?" (Acts 1:6)

Jesus responded by calling them to a new kingdom perspective, an eternal Kingdom that would flow out of the witness of His Name. He spoke of being His witnesses in the power of His Spirit. Then He was taken from their sight:

> And when he had said these things, as they were looking on, he was lifted up, and a cloud took him out of their sight. (Acts 1:9)

I am sure the disciples could hardly believe their eyes. They were not prepared for this at all! Then the angels of God gave them, and us, this glorious promise:

> And while they were gazing into heaven as he went, behold, two men stood by them in white robes, and said, "Men of Galilee, why do you stand looking into heaven? This Jesus, who was taken up from you into heaven, will come in the same way as you saw him go into heaven." (Acts 1:10-11)

Forty years later the Apostle Peter was writing his second letter. Even after such a brief period of time, people were responding just as that young man in Australia. They were asking the same question and answering in such a way that license was given to live the way they desired, apart from God and His holiness.

> knowing this first of all, that scoffers will come in the last days with scoffing, following their own sinful desires. They will say, "Where is the promise of his coming? For ever since the fathers fell asleep, all things are continuing as they were from the beginning of creation." (2 Peter 3:3-4)

THE PROMISES OF GOD ARE YES AND AMEN!

Jesus promised to return to this earth. How confident can we be in God's promises? The Apostle Paul talked to us about the promises of God in his second letter to the Church in Corinth:

> For all the promises of God find their Yes in him. That is why it is through him that we utter our Amen to God for his glory. (2 Corinthians 1:20)

Paul made this statement as he explained his own confidence in God's leading in his life. He had made a ministry decision that the Corinthians did not understand. In fact, it appears that they believed that Paul had missed God's leading after he had talked of visiting them on a trip to Macedonia and then again on his way back. When God led him another way, the church in Corinth questioned Paul's ability to hear the Lord clearly. In this context, Paul taught that the basis of his confidence was how he approached the Lord and his brothers and sisters in Corinth. He came before them in "simplicity and godly sincerity" and not in worldly wisdom (2 Cor. 1:12). In that confidence Paul walked with God in ministry, and in that confidence Paul listened to all of the promises of God.

THEY DELIBERATELY FORGET

Whereas the Apostle Paul based all of his life and ministry on his confidence in the Word of God and his Father's faithfulness in keeping His promises, most people in this world live in denial of the Scriptures. Remember that Peter is writing to "stir up our sincere mind." He wants us to recall the words spoken to us in earlier times by the prophets. But in contrast to the people of God who live with a mindset of God's Word, others in this world try to put out of their minds the words that God has spoken:

> For they deliberately overlook this fact, that the heavens existed long ago, and the earth was formed out of water and through water by the word of God, (2 Peter 3:5)

The scoffers who question the coming of the Lord deliberately forget that this world was created by the Word of God! They choose not to remember that God spoke this world into existence by the creative power of His voice. The Apostle Paul also talked of those who refuse to believe the truth of the Word of God:

> For the wrath of God is revealed from heaven against all ungodliness and unrighteousness of men, who by their unrighteousness suppress the truth. For what can be known about God is plain to them, because God has shown it to them. (Romans 1:18-19)

God's wrath is prepared for those who suppress the truth that He reveals. Why do they suppress His truth? Because of their own wickedness! God made plain to everyone in this world the truths of His existence and His glory in His own creation. We can look at what was made and know that a God of power, intelligence and design is behind it all. It is obvious that a Person made what exists because God has shown His personality and His attributes in the order, the colors, the smells, the sounds, and the beauty of His creation:

> For his invisible attributes, namely, his eternal power and divine nature, have been clearly perceived, ever since the creation of the world, in the things that have been made. So they are without excuse. (Romans 1:20)

What God desires us to know about Him, to prepare us to respond to further revelations of Himself in His Word and in His Son, is spectacularly and gloriously put on display in His creation. All of it has been clearly seen, and we are without excuse. But, as Paul said, ungodly people suppress that truth in their wickedness.

As Paul continues his teaching, he talks of those who exalt themselves even as they are rejecting the truth about God (verses

21-25). Why do wicked people suppress the truth about God and exalt themselves? First of all, of course, it is because they have listened to the lies about God that our enemy brings. Satan told Eve that through her rebellion and disobedience she would "be like God" (Gen. 3:5). Our responses to these lies and the illusions which flow from them are the beginning point of every false religion in this world and every "new age" theology which we have pursued. Apart from responding to God's truth, we will believe that we can be gods ourselves.

Secondly, people suppress the truth about God because if they responded, they would have to recognize His lordship over their lives. If God created and rules this world, then He also created and rules our lives. Those in rebellion against God reject not only Him, but any claim that He may have on their lives. They live in the lie and the illusion that they are their own god and, therefore, have the freedom to do as they please. In the process, however, they also deliberately forget that they must give an account of their lives, and that they will face His judgment throne.

Matthew Henry, in his famed commentary, describes the voice of the scoffers in this way:

> Our tongues are our own, and our strength and time, and who is lord over us? Who shall contradict or control us, or ever call us to account for what we say or do? And, as they scorn to be confined by any laws of God in their conversation, so neither will they bear that the revelation of God should dictate and prescribe to them what they are to believe; as they will walk in their own way, and talk in their own language, so they will also think their own thoughts,

and form principles altogether their own: here also their own lusts shall be consulted by them.[2]

EXALTED ABOVE ALL

Why can we be confident in God's promises? Because of the nature of God's Word! God has placed His Word above all, lifted high along with His Name. He desires that exaltation to create within our hearts a sense of exultation as we bow in His presence in worship. Notice how the psalmist links God's love and faithfulness with the praise of His Name and His Word:

> I bow down toward your holy temple and give thanks to your name for your steadfast love and your faithfulness, for you have exalted above all things your name and your word. (Psalm 138:2)

King David worshiped the name of the Lord when God gave him victory over his enemies. Again we see how God's care and protection for His children are connected to the nature of the Word of the Lord:

> This God—his way is perfect; the word of the LORD proves true; he is a shield for all those who take refuge in him. (2 Samuel 22:31)

The psalmist also talked of the eternal nature of the Word of God. When God speaks a word, it is settled forever in heaven:

> Forever, O LORD, your word is firmly fixed in the heavens. (Psalm 119:89)

When we see how highly God reveres His Word and how the spoken Word of God endures forever, we can see why Peter has such confidence that God will keep His promise in The Day of the

---

[2]Matthew Henry's Commentary, vol. 6, (McLean, VA: MacDonald Publishing Co.), p. 1052.

Lord. The same God who spoke creation into being by His Word will fulfill His Word also in the return of His Son and the destruction of His enemies.

CREATION AND THE FLOOD

Peter not only uses creation as evidence for God's faithfulness to His Word, he uses the example of the Flood as well. By the Word of the Lord the heavens and the earth were formed "out of water and through water" (2 Pet. 3:5), and by the same Word the waters that were used in creation were used in the Flood:

> and that by means of these the world that then existed was deluged with water and perished. (2 Peter 3:6)

By the Word of the Lord, the Flood also came upon the earth, bringing destruction to all mankind. Peter then tells us that the Word which brought creation into being and brought the deluge of the Flood will also bring fire, judgment and destruction upon the ungodly:

> But by the same word the heavens and earth that now exist are stored up for fire, being kept until the day of judgment and destruction of the ungodly. (2 Peter 3:7)

There are many in this world who question the scriptural record of creation and the Flood. Some, even in our churches, would not look at the first seven chapters of Genesis as accurate history. Now we know that the Bible is not primarily a history book. It is a redemptive revelation of the Person of God. The Bible shows the heart of God as He is restoring a people to Himself, sending His own Son to take away the sins of all who will place their faith in Him. It tells us of the building of the Church of the Lord Jesus and a Kingdom that will never pass away. Even though it is not primarily historical in its nature, however, where the Bible touches history, we can trust completely in its veracity:

> By the word of the LORD the heavens were made, and by the breath of his mouth all their host. (Psalm 33:6)

God did create the world at a point in time. The heavens, the earth, and all that is in them were called into being by the Word of God. The book of Genesis reveals the beginning in this way:

> In the beginning, God created the heavens and the earth. The earth was without form and void, and darkness was over the face of the deep. And the Spirit of God was hovering over the face of the waters. (Genesis 1:1-2)

Thus begins the six days of Creation recorded for us in Genesis chapter one. When nothing else existed but God Himself, God caused the world as we know it to exist. He created the heavens and the earth. How did He do it? God fulfilled creation by the Word of His mouth:

> And God said, "Let there be light," and there was light. (Genesis 1:3)

DID THE FLOOD REALLY HAPPEN?

This same pattern is followed for all six days of creation. We see the same phrase repeated again and again: "and God said." "God said," and the heavens, the earth and all that is in them were brought into being! The same Word that fulfilled creation brought about the destruction in the great Flood that resulted in the death of every person, except for Noah and his family:

> Then the LORD said to Noah, "Go into the ark, you and all your household, for I have seen that you are righteous before me in this generation. (Genesis 7:1)

God told Noah to bring into the ark some of every living creature in order that they might be saved. In the midst of the evil that
had come to consume mankind, God desired to preserve His creation. He began that preservation with the righteous man Noah,
and then, after more preparation, the Flood would come:

> For in seven days I will send rain on the earth forty days and forty
> nights, and every living thing that I have made I will blot out from
> the face of the ground. (Genesis 7:4)

As I mentioned earlier, even believers sometimes question
the historical accuracy of the Bible's record of creation and the
Flood. We must know that this doubt not only calls into question
the inspiration of Scripture, it puts in question our confidence in
the Second Coming of Christ. Peter links his confidence in God's
promise concerning the return of our Lord on the record of both
the Flood and creation. Henry Morris addresses this issue in this
way:

> Even conservative Christians, although professing belief
> in the divine inspiration of Scripture, have often ignored
> the significance of the Flood. They have been intimidated
> by the evolutionary geologists and paleontologists who, for
> over a hundred years, have insisted that all of earth his-
> tory should be explained in terms of slow development
> over great ages by the operation of the same natural pro-
> cesses which now prevail, completely rejecting the concept
> of the universal Flood at the dawn of history. Many Chris-
> tians have attempted to work out a compromise with evo-
> lutionary geology by explaining the Flood as a local flood,
> caused by a great overflow of the Euphrates or some other
> river in the Middle East. It must be settled here, therefore,

first of all, that the Bible record does describe a universal, world-destroying Flood.[3]

The God who created the worlds by the power of His Word and brought about the Flood by the power of His Word is the same God who will fulfill the Second Coming of Christ in The Day of the Lord. If we take the first nine chapters of Genesis out of the Bible, or do not believe that the events described there happened exactly as described and within the time frame given, we will have no confidence that God will keep His promise in the return of His Son.

WE WILL STAND

The same God who brought about creation and the Flood by His Word has promised that The Day of the Lord will come. The present heavens and earth are reserved for fire in preparation for the new heavens and the new earth. The world in which we live is being kept for judgment and the destruction of ungodly men. This will happen in history, just as the creation and the Flood are historic events. But, for the children of God, we have other promises. I want to look at some of the promises our Father provides for His own in the midst of a world that is passing away.

Every generation of Christians since the Apostle John has believed that Jesus would, or could, return in its lifetime. That knowledge gives us hope in a world of terror, affliction and pain. When everything around us seems to change, we as God's children can live securely and serve Him with a whole heart. That wonderful truth is one of the promises given through the psalmist:

---

[3]Henry M. Morris, *The Genesis Record* (Grand Rapids, MI: Baker Book House, 1970), p. 199.

> God is our refuge and strength, a very present help in trouble.
> Therefore we will not fear though the earth gives way, though the
> mountains be moved into the heart of the sea, though its waters
> roar and foam, though the mountains tremble at its swelling.
> *Selah.* (Psalm 46:1-3)

This is the very teaching on which we build our lives! This is
why we can rest securely when we are attacked from every side
and we do not know what will confront us tomorrow. When so
many of the things in which we have hoped in this world are removed, where do we go? Our refuge is God. He is the stronghold
to which we run. He is the place of protection and security for
those who trust in Him. He is the strength we need when ours is
gone, and God alone will remain present every moment as our
Helper.

We could paraphrase verse two of Psalm 46, "Even if the entire earth crumbles and falls away, we will not be moved!" How
can we not be moved when everything around us has been
shaken? Because in the end, when everything else has been destroyed, our God will stand, and all who have placed their faith in
Christ will stand in Him.

Even Job, who suffered so much pain and confusion when
his world was crumbling around him, had this same hope in the
God who held him in His sovereign hands. God made promises to
Job that Job knew He would fulfill on the last day. Our Father
made the same promises to you and me:

> For I know that my Redeemer lives, and at the last he will stand
> upon the earth. And after my skin has been thus destroyed, yet
> in my flesh I shall see God, whom I shall see for myself, and my
> eyes shall behold, and not another. My heart faints within me!
> (Job 19:25-27)

WE WILL MAKE OUR HOME WITH YOU

Just before Jesus went to the cross, He called His disciples to trust Him. He had told them that He was going away and that they could not go with Him. Their hopes were so wrapped in His personal presence with them that they could hardly bear these words. He then gave them this amazing promise:

> Let not your hearts be troubled. Believe in God; believe also in me. In my Father's house are many rooms. If it were not so, would I have told you that I go to prepare a place for you? And if I go and prepare a place for you, I will come again and will take you to myself, that where I am you may be also. (John 14:1-3)

Jesus is preparing a place for you and me in the Father's house! We have a home that is being made ready for us, perfectly fit for our hearts. Karen and I moved into a new home just a few months ago, and we watched with great delight as the builder built it according to our specifications. We designed it thoughtfully so that we could find rest and enjoyment there. It turned out just the way we wanted it to be. We love every moment we can spend in our home because it is ours, the very place we feel the most comfortable and secure. When we are away on a trip, we long to return home. But this is a home fit only for this world!

The home that Jesus is preparing for us is even more beautiful! It is in the Father's house, but it will be our home. That is where our hearts long to be; we yearn to go there after a brief journey in this world. Our glorious Lord will come back for us and take us home.

Jesus made another promise to His disciples that, if it could be possible, seems even more wonderful than the first. While we are still in this world, He and His Father will come and live with us here:

> Jesus answered him, "If anyone loves me, he will keep my word, and my Father will love him, and we will come to him and make our home with him. (John 14:23)

God has given us His presence even while we are living in this world, and in His presence we possess a second future filled with hope. As children of our Heavenly Father, we live securely and freely, even in a troubled world where terror would steal our hope and peace away. We face tomorrow confidently because the God in whom we rest today holds all of our tomorrows in His sovereign hands.

It was during a time of slavery and exile that God spoke to His people through the prophet Jeremiah. They had faced terrible enemies and had lost almost everything in this world. They had no reason, other than the glorious God who had made them His own, to live with even a glimmer of hope in this world. The promise of God to them is His promise to you and me this very day:

> For I know the plans I have for you, declares the LORD, plans for wholeness and not for evil, to give you a future and a hope. (Jeremiah 29:11)

When we understand that God is our hope and our future, our hearts will be drawn to Him, and we will trust in Him rather than in the things of this world wherein we have placed our hopes. The more we realize that this earth is not our home, the more we will seek the Lord. This is part of the process our God uses to turn our hearts toward Him so that we might seek Him and be found by Him:

> Then you will call upon me and come and pray to me, and I will hear you. You will seek me and find me. When you seek me with all your heart, I will be found by you, declares the LORD, and I will restore your fortunes and gather you from all the nations and all

the places where I have driven you, declares the LORD, and I will bring you back to the place from which I sent you into exile. (Jeremiah 29:12-14)

God promised His children a "hope and a future." There is nothing in this world—no political system, war or threat—that can steal away from us the hope He brings. Let's purpose to seek Him and to be found in Him who alone can protect us and preserve us for the Day of His coming:

For I am sure that neither death nor life, nor angels nor rulers, nor things present nor things to come, nor powers, nor height nor depth, nor anything else in all creation, will be able to separate us from the love of God in Christ Jesus our Lord. (Romans 8:38-39)

GROUP STUDY GUIDE
AND PERSONAL APPLICATION

1. Have you fallen into the skepticism that causes you to question whether Jesus will actually return to earth? Why or why not?

2. Are there those in your family or group of friends who "deliberately forget," or suppress the truth that God reveals? Why do you think they do this?

3. God talks about His Word being perfect, flawless and eternal. What are the implications of that for your life from day to day?

4. Peter links our confidence in Christ's return to the fact that God created the world by His Word and brought the Flood by His Word. How do you look at the first nine chapters of Genesis?

5. What do we lose if the first nine chapters of Genesis are only allegories rather than historical truth? What is jeopardized if these

are just stories which provide an understanding of how this world and mankind began?

6. God promised that when everything around us is shaking, He would be an "ever present helper." Has He kept that promise in your life? How has He done that?

7. Just before Christ returned to His Father, He promised that He would prepare a place for us to live with Him. Then He promised that He and His Father would come and live with us where we live. What difference does the presence of God make in your life from day to day?

8. God told His people that He had plans for them, plans that were good, providing a future and a hope. We will be looking at Peter's teaching about this world being destroyed. Do you face the future with confidence and hope? Why or why not?

REFLECTIONS, COMMITMENTS AND PRAYER

Perhaps you have questioned whether God keeps His promises in His Word and have fallen into the skepticism of our culture. Ask God to give you a renewed confidence in His promises. Thank Him for the promise of His presence in your life in every situation. Spend some moments in personal worship, thanking God for the hope He has promised you in the future no matter what takes place in the world around you.

The revelation of Jesus Christ, which God gave him to show to his servants the things that must soon take place. He made it known by sending his angel to his servant John,

Revelation 1:1

2

When Will Jesus Return? Soon!

As we studied in the first chapter, the promises of God are the basis for our confidence as His children. All of our hope is in God who keeps His promises! The Apostle John, writing some sixty years after Jesus' return to His Father, was convinced that Jesus would keep His promise to return:

> The revelation of Jesus Christ, which God gave him to show to his servants the things that must soon take place. He made it known by sending his angel to his servant John, who bore witness to the word of God and to the testimony of Jesus Christ, even to all that he saw. (Revelation 1:1-2)

Even those who believe with all their hearts that Jesus will keep His promise and return for His own often ask the question, "*When* will His Second Coming take place. *When* will Jesus return?" John answers that question for us: He is coming soon! The apostles and disciples of the Lord Jesus who lived in the first century believed that Jesus would return in their lifetimes. Our Father desires us to live with that same sense of expectation. We, too, must live in light of our Lord's Second Advent, which is very near:

> Blessed is the one who reads aloud the words of this prophecy, and blessed are those who hear, and who keep what is written in it, for the time is near. (Revelation 1:3)

As the Apostle John closed his revelation of Jesus Christ, he quoted the Lord Himself. Jesus affirms His soon return:

> And behold, I am coming soon. Blessed is the one who keeps the words of the prophecy of this book. (Revelation 22:7)

Sometimes, like that young man in Australia, we settle into thinking that the promises of Christ's return were given so many thousands of years ago and nothing has really changed. "Everything goes on as it has before, so why should I live each moment as if He might come today?" This is an honest question and a great challenge for us who love the Lord and desire to live as His servants. The truth is that everything in our lives will be determined by our view of Jesus' return. Our hunger for holiness, our attitudes toward our marriage partners and our families, how we view our time and our money will all be determined by whether we believe that Jesus will return soon. If we believe that His return is imminent, that Jesus could come back today, we will pursue Him and His Kingdom with all of the passions of our hearts. If not, we will live as the children of this world.

Again, John uses the very words of our Lord to close his Revelation of Jesus Christ. The testimony, which He Himself gives, is that "He is coming soon." May our response be that of His beloved apostle: "Yes! Come soon!"

> He who testifies to these things says, "Surely I am coming soon." Amen. Come, Lord Jesus! (Revelation 22:20)

The Scriptures clearly teach that Jesus Christ will return to this earth to receive His own and to reign in His glory. It will be the very event that fulfills history and our lives as well. It will surely take place in the realms of time and space on a date set by the Father. Christ's return could come today or tomorrow. But if Jesus does not return before we die, it will take place for you and me when we fall asleep in Jesus and awaken in the glorious eternal "now" in which God is summing up all things in His Son. We will come back to that exciting truth later in this chapter.

AN ETERNAL FOCUS

We have talked of the difficulties that confront us continually in this world. How can we possibly keep from losing heart in the midst of the terrible pain and loss that we face from day to day? The Apostle Paul taught the church at Corinth the glorious realities of the Christian life, a life which is lived out in triumph in the very face of a world that is passing away:

> So we do not lose heart. Though our outer nature is wasting away, our inner nature is being renewed day by day. (2 Corinthians 4:16)

We do not lose heart, Paul says, because even though we are "wasting away" physically, God is renewing our inner person from day to day. Paul's own persecutions were so great at this time that he said he "despaired even of life, and felt the sentence of death" (2 Cor. 1:8-9). Sometimes the circumstances that we face are so devastating that we feel we cannot go on for even one more day. But God tells us that His grace is there each moment to fill us up and sustain us no matter what we face. What God does within us is in complete contrast to what is taking place around us! Then Paul shares with us his incredible eternal perspective:

45

> For this slight momentary affliction is preparing for us an eternal weight of glory beyond all comparison, (2 Corinthians 4:17)

The afflictions that we face are "momentary and slight," Paul says. What are these momentary and light troubles? Our difficulties surely do not feel that way when we are going through them! I think Paul is describing the totality of life in this world. In the midst of the many joys that our Father provides for us, in this present world we face one difficulty after another. We face sickness and financial pressures. We confront loneliness and even rejection. Emotional battles and spiritual warfare are a day-to-day reality. Our relationships often bring much pain in the midst of their joy; sometimes confusion and despair would overwhelm us.

But Paul says these are only momentary. We want to cry out, "When these troubles go on for months and even years, how can you call them momentary?" Because there is a glimmer of eternal reality in the midst of it all! God gave Paul the ability to see beyond the level of human experience to the eternal glory that God was fulfilling even in the face of His painful experiences. He not only fills us up and renews us every day as we confront the devastation of this world, God builds eternal things into us in the very process. The glorious work that God is doing in us now and preparing for us in the future far outweighs the pain and loss we are experiencing now.

The process that God is fulfilling in us now is preparing us for eternity. There is glory ahead of us, incredible things awaiting us. The trouble we face now is nothing compared to the glory we will enjoy when we are with the Lord! What is the eternal glory that Paul is talking about? Surely, the glory will be focused on seeing the face of our beloved Lord. It will be wonderful to see loved ones that have gone before us to be with the Lord. Hearing the words "well done, good and faithful servant" will be glorious. The work that God prepared for us as we serve Him in eternity will also be filled with glory, and the worship before His throne of glory will fulfill every purpose of our creation. Those eternal glories will outweigh any afflictions we endure along the way in this world.

> as we look not to the things that are seen but to the things that are unseen. For the things that are seen are transient, but the things that are unseen are eternal. (2 Corinthians 4:18)

Paul's response, then, to this moving revelation from God became an eternal vision that moved him in all of his ministry. Because of the eternal weight of glory that he had seen, Paul's eyes were focused on what was eternal rather than on what was temporal. That is how he would live for the remainder of his days on this earth, with his eyes fixed on the new heaven and earth and his heart yearning for eternity.

AN EARTHLY TENT: AN ETERNAL HOUSE

What does it mean for Paul to "fix his eyes on what is unseen?" It means an increasing desire to be present with the Lord he loves and to be released from his body that is fitted for this world. He continues in his letter to the Corinthians by contrasting an "earthly tent" with an "eternal house:"

> For we know that if the tent, which is our earthly home, is destroyed, we have a building from God, a house not made with hands, eternal in the heavens. (2 Corinthians 5:1)

Paul knows that someday his earthly body will be destroyed, along with everything else designed for this realm of time. But he also knows that it will not be the end of life, and he is filled with hope! When our earthly tent is destroyed, we have a building from God. He refers to both of these as *dwelling places*. We live in a tent now, but someday we will live in an eternal house. What a contrast we see here between a temporary experience and an eternal one! Karen and I have some good friends who lived in a tent in their backyard while they were building their new house. Can you imagine how difficult it would be living under those conditions for several months? They were so grateful when they moved into their new house which had all of the facilities needed for a comfortable and secure life in this world:

> For in this tent we groan, longing to put on our heavenly dwelling, if indeed by putting it on we may not be found naked. (2 Corinthians 5:2-3)

Paul is addressing our "comfort levels" here. Just as our friends were feeling out of place and uncomfortable living in their tent, Paul was uncomfortable living in his temporal body. When Paul came to know Christ as his Savior and Lord, he became an eternal person. The more he knew Christ, the more he hungered for eternity and the more uncomfortable he became living in a body fit for a temporal experience. In fact, he more than hungered; he *longed* and he *groaned.*

WE WILL NOT BE UNCLOTHED

In this passage, Paul expresses confidence but also concern. Paul does not want to be found naked; he desires to be clothed. There seems to be a real level of comfort in Paul's heart that he will not be in a state of being "unclothed"—that is, in a state of being without a body. He not only groans as he longs to be clothed with his "heavenly dwelling;" he appears to be relieved that he will not be unclothed in between. He does not want to be naked:

> For while we are still in this tent, we groan, being burdened—not that we would be unclothed, but that we would be further

clothed, so that what is mortal may be swallowed up by life. (2 Corinthians 5:4)

Paul not only expresses a sense of "groaning," a deep anxious longing, while he is in his physical body; he describes a "burden" that his heart is carrying. The burden is the fear of being un-clothed. So, in Paul's heart there is a longing for his heavenly body and a burden of not wanting to be found naked. Then he sets before us the graphic picture of what is mortal, or dying in this world, being "swallowed up" by life. Someday, the new resur-rection body that will be ours when Christ returns will swallow up this dying body which is our tent in this world.

He who has prepared us for this very thing is God, who has given us the Spirit as a guarantee. (2 Corinthians 5:5)

God, who always keeps His Word, has given us a pledge that what He promised will come true. In fact, He guaranteed it! How do we know that what Paul is teaching us concerning an eternal glory and a heavenly body will actually take place? God gives us the eternal power and reality of His Holy Spirit even while we are presently living in this world in a temporal body. The Holy Spirit is our connection to eternity while we are living in a world that is passing away. He is also our heavenly source of life and power, enabling us to live on an eternal level even while we are physically present in the realms of time and space:

So we are always of good courage. We know that while we are at home in the body we are away from the Lord, for we walk by faith, not by sight. (2 Corinthians 5:6-7)

Paul views the body as a barrier. It separates us from being with the Lord. All of the things that we believe now about the Kingdom of God and enjoying the Lord's presence we do by faith. As intimate and real as our relationship with Christ may be now, it is not one of "sight;" we are not seeing His face presently. Our hearts are filled with the faith that one day we will enjoy the reality of our Lord's presence and see His face. But while we are in this body, we are away from the Lord:

> Yes, we are of good courage, and we would rather be away from the body and at home with the Lord. So whether we are at home or away, we make it our aim to please him. (2 Corinthians 5:8-9)

Paul's life and ministry were based on his confidence in the truths that he is teaching us now. These are the eternal things that God has given him the grace to see even in the midst of temporal experiences and momentary troubles, and he wants us to see them, too. Paul's deepest desire is to be with the Lord, but he knows that as long as he is here, at home in his body, he will be away from the Lord. He wants to be away from his body so that he can be at home with his Lord. This is the fruit of living intimately with the Lover of his soul even while present in this world. His life goal is not to "get to heaven," but to please the Lord. Whether in this body or with the Lord, Paul's desire is to live a life that brings pleasure to the God He serves:

> For we must all appear before the judgment seat of Christ, so that each one may receive what is due for what he has done in the body, whether good or evil. (2 Corinthians 5:10)

This section of teaching closes with a call to stewardship. We will all appear before the judgment seat of Christ. Each one of us will stand before the *judgment seat* or *reward bar* of our great and glorious God and receive what is due us for what we have done while we are here in this world, living in our physical bodies. This will not be a judgment of our souls, for Christ took our judgment at the cross. His blood was shed for our sins, and by faith we have believed in His eternal work at Calvary to take us to God. Paul is talking here about a judgment of our actions in this world, the works that we have done while in this body. We will have to give an account of our lives.

What hope the Scriptures bring us! Someday soon we will be released from this earthly tent that has been our body in this world, and we will be with our glorious Lord. We will receive a new dwelling, a heavenly one. What was mortal will be swallowed up in life, and we will not be unclothed. We will no longer groan, but we will worship. And all of the momentary troubles that we have suffered will be forgotten in the midst of the eternal glory that far outweighs them all. And it will all happen soon!

DEATH IS NOT OUR FRIEND

It is interesting to me that Paul is not describing death here as the hope of his life. He is not looking forward to dying; he is looking forward to being clothed with his new body and being present with his Lord. We sometimes talk of death as our friend in this world, as if it brings us hope. For example, a loved one who is suffering great pain might look forward to death as a release. But the Bible does not describe death as a friend; it talks of death as an enemy. When Paul wrote his first Corinthian letter, he pictured Christ's triumph and reign in this way:

> For he must reign until he has put all his enemies under his feet. The last enemy to be destroyed is death. (1 Corinthians 15:25-26)

Death is not our friend; death is our enemy. Our hope for ourselves or our loved ones who are suffering is not that we will die but that we will share in the triumph of our God who has defeated our terrible enemy. That defeat comes not in our death but in the resurrection. This teaching comes from Paul in the midst of his

51

defense of the resurrection of Christ and our resurrection in Him on the last day.

I will never forget the overwhelming pain and anguish our family experienced when we lost our nephew Kenny in a terrible train accident. He was only fifteen years old and a beautiful young man who trusted in the Lord. My dear sister Kathy and her husband Ken did not see death as a friend! The anger, confusion and grief continued to wash over their hearts for many months. Even now, years later, not many days go by without their thinking of Kenny and being reminded of their incredibly painful loss. Our great "Father of mercies and God of all comfort" has healed and carried them, and their faith in Christ has sustained them. Their hope is in the resurrection when they will be reunited with Kenny, and their joy in the Lord will be so great that they wouldn't change one thing about the Father's process:

> But if there is no resurrection of the dead, then not even Christ has been raised. And if Christ has not been raised, then our preaching is in vain and your faith is in vain. (1 Corinthians 15:13-14)

Our faith and all of our ministries are based on the resurrection of Christ. This world talks often about the "moral teachings of Jesus" as the heart of Christianity. The world might debate whether the resurrection really happened, but what the world thinks is really important is that we follow His life of love and peace. Whether Jesus was who He claimed to be, the Son of God, isn't really as important as the teachings He left us. This perspective must be rejected for what it is: false religion! Without the resurrection, there is no Christianity. If Jesus is not the Son of God, then He is a liar and not worthy of our following, much less our worship.

In his excellent book, *Why Believe?*, C. Stephen Evans confronts the reality of Jesus' claims and our responses to them in this world. He tells of a conversation years ago on the *Dick Cavett Show* between Jane Fonda and the Archbishop of Canterbury. "Jesus is the Son of God, you know," the Archbishop said. Jane Fonda responded, "Maybe He is for you, but He's not for me." The Archbishop retorted "Well, either He is or He isn't."[4]

In this world of relativism, pluralism, and tolerance, there remains objective truth that we can build our lives upon. One of those foundational realities is the resurrection of Jesus Christ from the dead. Paul bases his teaching not on Jesus' sincerity, His personal goodness, or the beautiful principles He left us to live by. The bedrock of our faith is that God actually, at a point in history, raised Jesus from the dead.

Our Hope Is in the Resurrection

For if the dead are not raised, not even Christ has been raised. And if Christ has not been raised, your faith is futile and you are still in your sins. Then those also who have fallen asleep in Christ have perished. (1 Corinthians 15:16-18)

Our hope as the children of God is in the resurrection. Christ was raised, and we will be raised! Our faith is not futile, and we are no longer in our sins. This confidence is for ourselves and for those we love who have fallen asleep in Jesus. They have not been lost. We will be reunited with them in the resurrection; we will see their faces again. Our joy in one another and in our triumphant Lord will be far beyond any human experience and beyond our ability to describe it:

---

[4]C. Stephen Evans, *Why Believe?*, (Grand Rapids, MI: William B. Eerdmans Publishing Co., 1996), p. 137.

> If in this life only we have hoped in Christ, we are of all people most to be pitied. (1 Corinthians 15:19)

Christ is our life, our strength and our joy in this world. He is the One who sustains us from day to day with all of the eternal resources of His life. But, as Paul says here, if He is our hope in this life alone, then we are in fact without hope. Knowing Christ in this world brings us incredible peace and joy, but the fullness of our hope is focused in the resurrection where we will be raised in Christ to life everlasting and the glories of eternity.

WE WILL BE CHANGED!

The resurrection is our entry experience into God's heavenly realm. We cannot enter eternity with our flesh and blood bodies. Our physical body must be changed to an eternal body in order to enter the heavenlies, and that is what takes place in the resurrection. Paul talked about that later in this same chapter:

> I tell you this, brothers: flesh and blood cannot inherit the kingdom of God, nor does the perishable inherit the imperishable. (1 Corinthians 15:50)

Our bodies in this world are "perishable;" they are passing away. We are dying. Only what is eternal will be able to exist in eternity, and so we need an imperishable body before we can function in God's new heaven and new earth. God has designed us for eternity, but we must be changed from mortal to immortal to experience it. We are eternal persons who have shared a brief, temporal experience:

> Behold! I tell you a mystery. We shall not all sleep, but we shall all be changed, in a moment, in the twinkling of an eye, at the last trumpet. For the trumpet will sound, and the dead will be raised imperishable, and we shall be changed. (1 Corinthians 15:51-52)

Surely, what Paul is teaching us here is a great mystery! Not every one of us will fall asleep in this world and experience death, as Christ may come for us before we die. But our bodies will all be changed from mortal to immortal bodies. When the last trumpet sounds, in the "twinkling of an eye," those of us who have died will be changed. Our mortal bodies will be transformed and become imperishable:

> For this perishable body must put on the imperishable, and this mortal body must put on immortality. When the perishable puts on the imperishable, and the mortal puts on immortality, then shall come to pass the saying that is written: "Death is swallowed up in victory." (1 Corinthians 15:53-54)

These are incredibly visual pictures that Paul is painting for us here: the perishable clothing itself with the imperishable and the mortal with the immortal. This reminds us of Paul's teaching in 2 Corinthians 5 where he cries out about not wanting to be "unclothed." We, too, hunger to be "clothed" with our eternal bodies. And then Paul describes death being "swallowed up" in victory. How often have we stood at the coffin of a loved one and felt overwhelmed with our grief and loss? It seems that the pain of that devastating experience overtakes all of our hopes and our joys. But according to the Scriptures, that is not the end of the story. In the end, death itself will be swallowed up; it will be overwhelmed in the victory of the resurrection:

> O death, where is your victory? O death, where is your sting? (1 Corinthians 15:55)

The empty "victory" of death has been stolen away in the resurrection of Jesus Christ, and we share in the fullness of true victory when we are raised in Him. When we lay a loved one in the arms of Jesus, the sting, the pain, seems more than we can carry for even one more moment. Our hearts tell us that we will never rejoice again. Christ bore the sting of death for us in the cross, and in His triumph removed the "stinger" of our great enemy, Satan. Now, even though the pain of death seems almost unbearable to us, the sting of death has, in fact, been removed. We know that soon we will see our Lord and be reunited with our loved ones in the resurrection, and our joy will be uncontainable:

> The sting of death is sin, and the power of sin is the law. But thanks be to God, who gives us the victory through our Lord Jesus Christ. (1 Corinthians 15:56-57)

THE TRUMPET CALL OF GOD

The Apostle Paul returned to this theme as he wrote to the church at Thessalonica. In his first letter to them, he brought their hearts back to the hope of the resurrection. Concerning those who have fallen asleep, he says:

> But we do not want you to be uninformed, brothers, about those who are asleep, that you may not grieve as others do who have no hope. (1 Thessalonians 4:13)

Knowing the eternal realities of our temporal experiences sets us free to go through them differently than do the others of this world. When we understand the truth of our future in Christ and do not live ignorantly, we do not grieve as those who have no hope. Just as Paul did with his brothers and sisters at Corinth, he brings the hearts of his beloved friends in Thessalonica back to the historical record of Christ's resurrection:

> For since we believe that Jesus died and rose again, even so, through Jesus, God will bring with him those who have fallen asleep. (1 Thessalonians 4:14)

At a point in time, God raised Jesus from the dead. We believe that and confess it as the foundation of our faith. As Paul teaches us, it is also true that we will be raised in Him. He sets before us this picture of incredible glory: when Jesus returns, He will bring with Him all those who have "fallen asleep in Him:"

> For this we declare to you by a word from the Lord, that we who are alive, who are left until the coming of the Lord, will not precede those who have fallen asleep. (1 Thessalonians 4:15)

Placing our hope once again in the promises of God, Paul tells us that we who remain alive until the coming of the Lord will not "precede" our loved ones who have fallen asleep. As Paul said to the Corinthians, we will all be changed at the resurrection; but now he says that those who "sleep," who have died, will rise first:

> For the Lord himself will descend from heaven with a cry of command, with the voice of an archangel, and with the sound of the trumpet of God. And the dead in Christ will rise first. (1 Thessalonians 4:16)

This is the moment that we long for! When we lay a precious loved one in the grave, we long for this moment. When we suffer pain and afflictions in this world, we long for this moment. Jesus will enter time once again. Now He will come not as the Lamb of God to take away our sins, but as the exalted Lord of glory. He will come with a loud command, holding in Himself all of the authority in the universe. We will hear with our own ears the voice of Michael, the archangel. The trumpet call of God will summon us, and those who have died in Christ will be raised:

> Then we who are alive, who are left, will be caught up together with them in the clouds to meet the Lord in the air, and so we will always be with the Lord. (1 Thessalonians 4:17)

The Day of the Lord!

Then we who remain alive will join them. We, too, will be changed and meet the Lord in the air! Forever we will be with the Lord, reunited with our family, our friends and all of our brothers and sisters in this world who placed their faith in Christ.

We will meet the Lord! This is the fulfillment of every hope and longing we have ever experienced. We will see the face of our glorious Lord, the Lover of our soul, the One who pursued us even from eternity, and who laid down His life for us at the cross. He with whom we have shared such intimacy, who has shepherded us, guided us and protected us—we will see His face. We have hungered for His presence day after day in this world. We sought His face from a distance, and now we will be present with Him in an experience that far transcends our greatest dreams. Our life will be fulfilled in that moment, and an eternity of worship will begin.

> Therefore encourage one another with these words.
> (1 Thessalonians 4:18)

We need to remind each other of these words. We so easily lose sight of the eternal realities in the midst of our temporal experiences. As we carry the burdens and responsibilities of this life, we tend to think that these circumstances will never change. We will never be free from the temptations that relentlessly beckon our flesh; we will never get beyond the pain we bear; and, we will not get through the loneliness that haunts us. But remember, these are momentary and light afflictions. They are temporary and they are bearable because God is in the process with us. We live day by day with His power filling us and His presence surrounding us, and someday, very soon, we will see His face. And it will be worth it all. Let's keep encouraging each other with these words!

GOD AND TIME

I am convinced that from the Scriptures we can conclude when a believer dies, he or she immediately experiences the resurrection and the Second Coming of our Lord. This is my personal belief after studying these Scriptures for many years, and I encourage you to think and pray with me about these things. I come to this conclusion on the basis of Paul's confidence that there will be no time when he is "unclothed." The reality is that for the believer who dies, time is no more.

Let's go back to Paul's teaching in 2 Corinthians 5. He clearly says that to be absent from our body is to be present with the Lord. Yet when we lay a loved one in the grave, we know that according to the Scriptures they have fallen asleep in Him (1 Thes. 4:14). We often talk about them as if they are with the Lord now, but in fact, they do not yet have their eternal, resurrection bodies. How can they be asleep in Jesus and experiencing the glories of eternity at the same time? The answer lies in the amazing relationship between time and eternity which we are studying here.

When we look at the experience of death from the perspective of time, the person we buried is sleeping in Jesus awaiting the resurrection. But do you remember Paul's joy in knowing that he would not be unclothed; that is, in a state without a body, and would be immediately with the Lord? How can both be true? How can we, from the perspective of time see a person "sleeping" and from the perspective of eternity see a person immediately experience the resurrection? Both are true because there is not a time between death and the resurrection when we are "disembodied spirits" waiting for our resurrection bodies. There is not a time because there is no time! Those who have placed their faith in Christ and have died have been released from time and are living in eternity, where everything takes place "now." So, for the believers who die, the resurrection is an immediate reality; they see their loved ones and are with the Lord. It is in this moment of death that two realms have intersected one another, the realm of time and the realm of eternity.

The great Bible teacher and former pastor of Peninsula Bible Church in Palo Alto, California, Ray Stedman described it this way:

> But what is even more amazing is that in the experience of that believer, he does not leave anyone behind. All his loved ones who know Christ are there too, including his Christian descendants who were not even born yet when he died! Since there is no past or future in heaven, this must be the case. Even those who, in time, stand beside his grave and weep and then go home to an empty house, are, in his experience with him in glory.[5]

It is no wonder that Paul closed his teaching to the Thessalonians about the coming of the Lord with the statement, "Therefore encourage each other with these words." The more we place our hope in the resurrection, the more our hearts are being prepared for the Day of His Coming!

GROUP STUDY GUIDE
AND PERSONAL APPLICATION

1. Have you lived with the knowledge that Jesus might return to-day? How has that knowledge affected your day-to-day experiences and attitudes?

2. Why do you think that the only timing the Scriptures give to us for the Lord's return is "soon?"

---

[5]Ray Stedman, *Authentic Christianity*, (c. Elaine Stedman, 1996) ch.9, p. 6.

3. Paul talks to the church at Corinth about "looking at the things that are unseen." In your own life, what gives you the most difficulty as you seek to keep an eternal focus?

4. Do you sense that God is renewing your inner person even as your outer person is in the process of wearing down? How have you experienced that?

5. What does it mean to "groan" in your "earthly tent?" Do you think that this has to do mostly with sickness, aging and dying, or something even larger in significance?

6. When we see people in this world suffering in great pain and sickness, we often see death as their friend, as in providing relief from their suffering. Why do the Scriptures not refer to death as our friend?

7. When Paul talks about "death being swallowed up in victory," what is the first thing that comes to your mind?

8. What does it mean for the "sting of death" to be removed? How does that relate to the power of sin and the law?

9. When Paul discusses "the trumpet call of God," and how in the resurrection we will be reunited with our loved ones and live with the Lord forever, what images fill your mind and your heart?

10. How do you respond to the thoughts about God and time? What about the link between our death, the resurrection and the coming of the Lord?

The Day of the Lord!

Reflections, Commitments and Prayer

Take the one thing that God most significantly spoke to you about in this chapter and bring it back to Him in prayer. Ask Him to fill you with hope in His promise of the resurrection and your reunion with loved ones in Him who you will meet "in the air" when Jesus calls you home. Pray that God will give you His grace each day while you are "groaning" in this temporal body and to live with it as your servant while you are waiting for its redemption when the "trumpet call of God" summons you to Himself.

The Lord is not slow to fulfill his promise as some count slowness, but is patient toward you, not wishing that any should perish, but that all should reach repentance.

2 Peter 3:9

3

God's Heart for His World

There is no Scripture that more wonderfully expresses the heart of God than 2 Peter 3:9. He does not want anyone to perish; He desires everyone to come to repentance! What Peter is expressing here, of course, is not the decreed or ordained will of God. If it were, everyone would be saved. Peter is expressing God's glorious heart of patience, waiting for men and women everywhere to believe, to respond to the gospel of salvation. As God prepares us for the return of His Son, He will give us His heart to bring the message of repentance to His world. That heart will transform our commitments to missions and evangelism.

Peter teaches us in this chapter about judgment and "the destruction of the ungodly" (2 Peter 3:7). That will happen in The Day of the Lord. God's righteous justice and His holy wrath will be poured out on His enemies who have lived in rebellion against Him. But from the beginning of time, God has been the "eternal pursuer." He came into the Garden of Eden (Gen. 3:8-9), pursuing Adam and Eve when they had fallen in their sin and rebellion, and He pursued you and me all the way to the Cross, even in the death of His own Son. Our Father's heart desires reconciliation, redemption and salvation.

GOD IS NOT SLOW; HE IS PATIENT

This most glorious truth is expressed in the words of the Lord Jesus Himself. The Apostle John records this in his gospel:

> For God so loved the world, that he gave his only Son, that whoever believes in him should not perish but have eternal life. (John 3:16)

That is how much God loved this world that He made. This is how much He loved every person He created in His image. God gave the Son He loved so that any person who places his faith in Him would not die, or as Peter might say, "suffer destruction," but rather live forever. Then Jesus continues His teaching in this way:

> For God did not send his Son into the world to condemn the world, but in order that the world might be saved through him. Whoever believes in him is not condemned, but whoever does not believe is condemned already, because he has not believed in the name of the only Son of God. (John 3:17-18)

Jesus makes it clear in this Scripture that God did not send His Son into the world for the purpose of condemnation. God sent Jesus into this world as a means of redemption and life for all who would believe. Those who are condemned die because they refuse to believe. So, those who suffer the destruction that Peter is describing in The Day of the Lord do so because of their will, not because of God's will. He is not willing that they should perish; they themselves are willing that they should perish. The heart of God has cried out for repentance and reconciliation from the beginning, even to the point of giving the life of His own Son for the lives of His enemies (Rom. 5:6-11). Paul also expressed our Father's heart for salvation in this way as he wrote to the church at Rome:

> For there is no distinction between Jew and Greek; the same Lord is Lord of all, bestowing his riches on all who call on him. For "everyone who calls on the name of the Lord will be saved." (Romans 10:12-13)

When Peter teaches us about God's heart for everyone to come to repentance, he tells us that God is not slow in fulfilling His promise for Christ to return. When the scoffers cry out, "Where is this coming He promised?"—we know that God is waiting for many to be saved. Many years will have gone by between the promise of God and its fulfillment in The Day of the Lord, not because He is slow, but because He is patient.

Why is God waiting patiently to send His Son back to earth? He is waiting for our family members to be converted, for our co-workers and our neighbors to respond to the gospel, and for the nations to come to the knowledge of Christ and to worship Him. He does not want them to suffer the terrible destruction of The Day of the Lord. When we share God's heart for people, our zeal for missions and evangelism is transformed!

GOD IS OUTSIDE OF TIME

In our preceding chapter, we studied the relationship between time and eternity. We come to those thoughts once again as Peter teaches about the patience of the Lord. What we might consider "slow" in our timetable is, of course, right on time in God's sovereign process.

> But do not overlook this one fact, beloved, that with the Lord one
> day is as a thousand years, and a thousand years as one day.
> (2 Peter 3:8)

God looks at time in a completely different way than we do because He experiences time in a completely different way. What
might be a normal day's experience for you and me, for God
might actually be a thousand years. What in this world might be
measured in a millennium, might be in God's eternal framework
only one more day.

God is not bound by time. For us, time is a constraint. There
are things and circumstances that we long for, and we can hardly
wait for them to happen. Other things we dread, and it seems
that they come upon us relentlessly. We often feel pressured to
produce certain things in a given amount of time. God is not under that kind of pressure as He is sovereign over time. He holds
all of history and all of our times in His hands. Since God is in
control of time, He can be patient.

Dr. Martyn Lloyd-Jones, the great pastor and Bible teacher
from England, talked about this amazing truth in this way:

> God is eternal, God is above time. We must never think
> about God as being included in the time process or in the
> flux and movement of time and history. God is altogether
> above time. It is almost impossible for us to grasp such a
> thought and such a concept, and yet it is a very vital prin-
> ciple. We, being creatures of time, of necessity think in
> terms of time. God is altogether above and beyond and
> outside it, so that when we are thinking of the purposes of
> God, it is always dangerous to exaggerate the time ele-
> ment. God, Himself being eternal, is right outside it. To
> Him, a thousand years are but one day and one day as a

thousand years. In other words, He does not live at all in the realm, or in terms of, the time process.[6]

GOD'S HEART FOR HIS KINGDOM

God has placed us in time to bring the gospel to a lost world. Our great and merciful God patiently waits for people to come to repentance before He sends His Son back to this earth in the terrible Day of the Lord. He would give us His heart for His world. God would build into us as His people a patient longing for others to come to salvation. He would give us a zeal for missions and evangelism in order that we might passionately pursue the glory of God in fulfilling the Great Commission.

Let's go back to the promise that our Lord made to His disciples just before He returned to His Father. For forty days He had lived among them, teaching them further about the Kingdom of God. And then He said:

> And while staying with them he ordered them not to depart from Jerusalem, but to wait for the promise of the Father, which, he said, "you heard from me; for John baptized with water, but you will be baptized with the Holy Spirit not many days from now." (Acts 1:4-5)

Jesus' command was for His disciples to wait in Jerusalem for the power of the Holy Spirit to come upon them. But look at their response:

> So when they had come together, they asked him, "Lord, will you at this time restore the kingdom to Israel?" (Acts 1:6)

Christ is calling His disciples to seek the resources of His Spirit for the ministry He has set before them, and they are ask-

---

[6]Martyn Lloyd-Jones, *Expository Sermons on 2 Peter* (Carlisle, PA: The Banner of Truth Trust, 1983), p. 178.

ing about a political kingdom. The hopes of their hearts are still focused in this world! After rebuking them, Jesus turns them once again to the focus of His heart—His glory revealed in the building of His Church:

> He said to them, "It is not for you to know times or seasons that the Father has fixed by his own authority. But you will receive power when the Holy Spirit has come upon you, and you will be my witnesses in Jerusalem and in all Judea and Samaria, and to the end of the earth." (Acts 1:7-8)

Jesus instructed His disciples to not focus on the Father's timetable but on His agenda. God would give us His heart for evangelism and missions. If God would use us in the building of His Church, we, too, must have our vision turned from this world to His Kingdom. We, too, must learn to seek God for the resources of His Spirit in the ministries that He has set before us.

A KINGDOM BEYOND POLITICS

Just as with the disciples, we often lose our focus on what is eternal. Rather than placing all of our hopes in the building of God's Kingdom which will last forever, we become far too focused on this kingdom which is passing away. God is calling us to orient all our strength, time, money, and prayer around His glory seen in His Church and the advancement of His Kingdom, and yet our hearts so easily become lost in this world. We might lose our way with our love for things or our desires for temporal experiences. Or, it can happen with legitimate pursuits of justice and righteousness in this world which may be foundational to the heart of God and yet less than the building of His Church.

What was wrong with the disciples asking Jesus about restoring the kingdom to Israel? Didn't that reflect God's heart for

His chosen people? Christ told them that dates and times were the Father's prerogative and should be left with Him. Jesus then shifted the disciples' focus to two greater priorities: the power of His Spirit and being His witnesses to the ends of the earth. The disciples had not learned yet what Christ said as He testified before Pilate:

> Jesus answered, "My kingdom is not of this world. If my kingdom were of this world, my servants would have been fighting, that I might not be delivered over to the Jews. But my kingdom is not from the world." (John 18:36)

Jesus' Kingdom is not of this world; it is His reign in the hearts of men and women everywhere who place their hopes and their trust in Him. It is seen in God's rule over governments and history; it is revealed in His power over all the earth. Too often our churches have lost their vision for the gospel, missions and evangelism as they have become entrenched in political causes. As I mentioned earlier, it is legitimate, even critical, for us to be involved in the pursuit of righteousness and justice in this world. Ministries that help the poor, protect unborn children, and lift up the weak also reflect the heart of God and His Kingdom. Entire societies have been transformed throughout history, enslaved peoples have been set free, and the place of women has been elevated as God's people have brought the prophetic word of the Scriptures to bear on the consciences of governments.

However, the Church has too often linked the cause of the gospel with political agendas. In the United States we have seen some who marry conservative Christianity with conservative politics. In other countries the Church is viewed officially or unofficially as the state religion. Occasionally Christianity is linked with anti-government policies when the government is oppressive.

It is significant to note that Jesus and Paul, Peter, Luke and John did not fall into this trap. The Roman system of government was oppressive and was surely anti-Christian. Slavery and injustice confronted believers on a daily basis. Yet we do not see Jesus or His followers seeking to transform Roman society by means of political agendas. They saw the Kingdom of God as beyond politics and sought to transform people from the inside out by the indwelling life of Christ. Both Paul and the Lord Jesus called these transformed people to become good citizens of their nations. History shows us that righteous people affected societies by the fruit of their transformed lives.

As the people of God, we must never separate preaching the gospel from the call to righteousness which transforms societies. Both of these are necessary in the building of God's Kingdom. But that is God's Kingdom which is coming, which He is building—not an earthly political agenda. Nothing less will enable us to walk with God in the fulfillment of His great eternal purpose:

> For the earth will be filled with the knowledge of the glory of the LORD as the waters cover the sea. (Habakkuk 2:14)

At this time the Church of the Lord Jesus is the physical expression of His Kingdom in the midst of this world. Just as Christ did with His disciples in Acts chapter one, turning their focus from political kingdoms in this world to the fulfillment of His commission, the building of His Church, He will do with you and me. He will focus our eyes and our hearts on the power of His Holy Spirit enabling us to take the gospel to the ends of the earth.

THE ACTS OF THE HOLY SPIRIT

As we continue in the book of Acts, we see that the Holy Spirit gave direction to the building of Christ's Church as the people of God were filled with His life and power. On the Day of Pentecost,

God's Spirit invaded the upper room where the disciples were gathered, and then He invaded their lives. God gathered 120 of His people in that room, and at the same time He had gathered many thousands to Jerusalem from the entire known world. Through the gifts of the Holy Spirit, God enabled the disciples to speak in the languages of the many peoples gathered there:

> And they were amazed and astonished, saying, "Are not all these who are speaking Galileans? And how is it that we hear, each of us in his own native language? Parthians and Medes and Elamites and residents of Mesopotamia, Judea and Cappadocia, Pontus and Asia, Phrygia and Pamphylia, Egypt and the parts of Libya belonging to Cyrene, and visitors from Rome, both Jews and proselytes, Cretans and Arabians—we hear them telling in our own tongues the mighty works of God." (Acts. 2:7-11)

The Apostle Peter stood up and began to preach. In his sermon, he taught the Scriptures, quoting from the Old Testament. Peter was clearly placing his confidence in the Word of God and God's ability to bring those to Himself who would be saved. Peter brought truths from the prophet Joel, Psalm 16 and Psalm 110. He preached Christ from the ancient Scriptures, and God brought three thousand to salvation.

God continued to give gifts of great power to the apostles. As Peter and John worked miracles of healing, the leaders of the Jews grew more and more threatened. The disciples were persecuted, imprisoned and stoned. The gospel continued to spread as the believers were filled with joy, and God continued to build His Church.

We see Paul of Tarsus standing with the persecutors and giving hearty approval to the stoning of Stephen. After Stephen's death, an even greater persecution began to break out against the believers, but this was all under God's sovereign control.

> And Saul approved of his execution. And there arose on that day
> a great persecution against the church in Jerusalem, and they
> were all scattered throughout the regions of Judea and Samaria,
> except the apostles. Devout men buried Stephen and made great
> lamentation over him. But Saul was ravaging the church, and
> entering house after house, he dragged off men and women and
> committed them to prison. (Acts 8:1-3)

As the Christians were scattered, the gospel began to spread
to the surrounding nations. Even with the threat of imprisonment and death, Christianity was relentlessly taken to the Gentiles. Philip told the good news about the risen Christ to a eunuch
from Ethiopia. A Roman centurion named Cornelius, who served
with "the Italian regiment," was directed by the Lord in a vision to
send for the Apostle Peter. At the same time, Peter was receiving a
vision of his own. God was teaching him that everything that God
declared clean was clean. So when the Gentile Cornelius sent for
him, Peter was prepared to see Gentiles brought into the Church.
When Peter explained the gospel, Cornelius and those gathered
with him believed:

> While Peter was still saying these things, the Holy Spirit fell on
> all who heard the word. And the believers from among the cir-
> cumcised who had come with Peter were amazed, because the
> gift of the Holy Spirit was poured out even on the Gentiles. For
> they were hearing them speaking in tongues and extolling God.
> (Acts 10:44-46)

Meanwhile, Saul of Tarsus was converted. God was preparing
him to become Paul, the Apostle to the Gentiles. In the amazing
way that God built His new Church, the gospel of Christ continued to spread relentlessly. The church at Antioch became the
first missionary-sending church. Look at the incredible
multi-national and multiracial group that God had gathered for
that first commissioning service:

Now there were in the church at Antioch prophets and teachers, Barnabas, Simeon who was called Niger, Lucius of Cyrene, Manaen a member of the court of Herod the tetrarch, and Saul. While they were worshiping the Lord and fasting, the Holy Spirit said, "Set apart for me Barnabas and Saul for the work to which I have called them." (Acts 13:1-2)

As we study the book of Acts, we learn that church growth is God's work. He does it in His way, in His time, to His own glory alone. It cannot be contained; it cannot be controlled; it cannot be designed; it cannot be programed. Our part in the process is to watch and see what God is doing and then aggressively enter into what He is doing (John 5:16-20; 8:28-30).

POLITICAL SYSTEMS ARE IRRELEVANT

The book of Acts continues with the amazing works of the Holy Spirit as the Church of the Lord Jesus is built. We see the sovereignty of God put on display through a group of ordinary, uneducated men and women, and God used them to turn the world upside down. The way God fulfilled all of His will in the midst of the most hostile political and religious environment causes us to stand in awe and worship before Him.

When we look at the glorious work of God today in the building of His Church around the world, we stand in amazement once again. We see governments throughout history, and even today, that made themselves enemies of God and sought to destroy His work. History tells us, however, that God and His Church have stood triumphant through the ages and will triumph at the end of time.

The Pharaoh of Egypt enslaved the children of Israel in order to build his own kingdom. He despised the name of God and fought against His purposes. But Paul tells us in the book of Romans that Pharaoh was God's tool for God's purposes:

> For the Scripture says to Pharaoh, "For this very purpose I have raised you up, that I might show my power in you, and that my name might be proclaimed in all the earth." (Romans 9:17)

The very same thing can be said about Nero. Nero was the emperor of Rome during the great persecutions of the Early Church in the first century. Nero hated the name of Jesus and sought to erase it from the face of the earth. What was God's response? He named Nero as the chairman of the committee for the evangelism of the Roman Empire! It was under Nero's rule that the gospel of Christ spread throughout the entire known world.

As we look at the world today, we might be tempted to conclude that certain forms of government, or certain political systems, are more favorable to the growth of Christianity, while other political systems hinder the growth of the Church. Those of us in the developed nations might think that democracy would provide the best environment for churches to grow. We might even point to our "mega-churches" as examples for our argument. Others may argue that a "benevolent dictatorship" is the best system for church growth and point to nations in the world which are ruled in that way where the churches are growing tremendously. Many might conclude that governments that oppress the Church or restrict church growth would be a great hindrance to its progress.

But, in fact, none of these is true. God is sovereign over His Church, and political systems are irrelevant. By the resources of the same Holy Spirit we see at work in the book of Acts, God builds His Church in His time and in the way which brings Him the most glory. There are many places in the developed nations where democracy has ruled for many years and at the same time church attendance has been in consistent decline. In the United States, there has been no real church growth for many years, in spite of our endless seminars, management techniques and methods for church growth. In Latin America, Africa and Asia where there are many different forms of government, many churches are experiencing explosive growth. How can we explain this? There is only one explanation and that is God Himself. Jesus prophesied to Peter that His Church would be built, regardless of the obstacles which she might face because Jesus Himself would build His Church:

> And Jesus answered him, "Blessed are you, Simon Bar-Jonah! For flesh and blood has not revealed this to you, but my Father who is in heaven. And I tell you, you are Peter, and on this rock I will build my church, and the gates of hell shall not prevail against it. (Matthew 16:17-18)

THE GLORY OF GOD AND THE JOY OF THE NATIONS

What motivates us to share God's heart for His world? What purpose is big enough to move us to walk with Him in the building of His Church? The Psalmist tells us in his great call to the earth and to the nations:

> Oh sing to the LORD a new song; sing to the LORD, all the earth! Sing to the LORD, bless his name; tell of his salvation from day to day. Declare his glory among the nations, his marvelous works among all the peoples! (Psalm 96:1-3)

God has prepared a new song for His creation and for the peoples of the earth. It is a song that exalts His name and declares His salvation. The melodies flow with the sounds of God's glory, and the theme is the marvelous work of His hands:

> For great is the LORD, and greatly to be praised; he is to be feared above all gods. For all the gods of the peoples are worthless idols,

but the LORD made the heavens. Splendor and majesty are before him; strength and beauty are in his sanctuary. (Psalm 96:4-6)

Because of God's greatness, He alone is worthy to be praised. His presence produces awe, reverence and fear. The gods of this world are lifeless, but our God gave life to the heavens and the earth. Splendor and majesty flow from His throne and strength and glory fill His dwelling place. This is a God worthy of worship!

Ascribe to the LORD, O families of the peoples, ascribe to the LORD glory and strength! Ascribe to the LORD the glory due his name; bring an offering, and come into his courts! Worship the LORD in the splendor of holiness; tremble before him, all the earth! (Psalm 96:7-9)

Now, in light of who God is and what He has done, the only fitting response of the nations is to give Him the glory that is rightfully due His name. We have seen His glory. We have known His power and His might. That knowledge has produced in us a message that calls the earth and the nations to tremble before Him in worship, even as we do, and to praise His Name. The greatest manifestation of pride and the most grievous sin is when the nations keep for themselves the glory that rightfully belongs only to God:

Say among the nations, "The LORD reigns! Yes, the world is established; it shall never be moved; he will judge the peoples with equity." (Psalm 96:10)

This is the voice of missions and the call of the Church. The response of the nations in light of the greatness of our God and the justice with which He rules can be nothing less than "the Lord reigns!" Anything less than the worship of God is idolatry. When those from every tribe and tongue and people and nation gather before the glorious throne of God in the fullness of time, this will be the song we will sing. As we proclaim His worthiness, His power and His glory, we will shout together "the Lord reigns!"

> Let the heavens be glad, and let the earth rejoice; let the sea roar, and all that fills it; let the field exult, and everything in it! Then shall all the trees of the forest sing for joy before the LORD, for he comes, for he comes to judge the earth. He will judge the world in righteousness, and the peoples in his faithfulness. (Psalm 96:11-13)

When we proclaim the greatness of God, the joy of heaven is reflected in the gladness of the earth. We experience that joy when we stand in worship in the assembly of God's people. We are joined even now by all of creation in exulting in the God who has made us and who rules in righteousness and glory. He will judge the world in that righteousness and the peoples in His truth. We await that judgment and the fullness of His worship in The Day of the Lord.

This is a purpose big enough for our lives and a call worthy of our hearts. Only the glory of God and the joy of the nations can move us to walk with Him in His wondrous design to fill the earth with His glory. When we share the motivations of our Father's heart, we can then pray with authority for the advancement of His mission purpose:

> Ask of me, and I will make the nations your heritage, and the ends of the earth your possession. (Psalm 2:8)

GLORY AND GOSPEL

The glory of God is both our message and our motivation. The worship of our glorious God by the nations and the fulfillment of their joy in Him moves us to bring the gospel to the ends of the earth. There is another aspect of this truth revealed by the Lord Jesus in His prayer in the garden just before the cross. He prayed for the unity of His disciples in order that the world might believe in Him:

> I do not ask for these only, but also for those who will believe in me through their word, that they may all be one, just as you, Father, are in me, and I in you, that they also may be in us, so that the world may believe that you have sent me. (John 17:20-21)

There is great power in our relationships to communicate the gospel of Christ to the world. Jesus had told this truth to His disciples earlier in the Upper Room Discourse:

> A new commandment I give to you, that you love one another: just as I have loved you, you also are to love one another. By this all people will know that you are my disciples, if you have love for one another. (John 13:34-35)

Even more than the power of our preaching, the creativity of our programs and the greatness of our missions, our love for one another validates the gospel we are proclaiming. By the way we walk with one another, the world will know that we come from Jesus. Our Lord is returning to that theme now as He talks about our unity. By our oneness, the world will know that He has in fact been sent by the Father. That is the essence of the gospel:

> The glory that you have given me I have given to them, that they may be one even as we are one, I in them and you in me, that they may become perfectly one, so that the world may know that you sent me and loved them even as you loved me. (John 17:22-23)

What is it that unifies us? It is the glory of God! We need something far bigger than we are, or what we are doing, to bring us together. Only God's glory transcends ourselves and our own goals and dreams. How often in our churches do we struggle with pettiness, divisions, and gossip? We fall easily into battling with issues that separate us on a political level. We argue about buildings and programs. Churches can live for decades in these places. Why do we do this? Because we do not share with one another something bigger than we are. We do not own a purpose higher than ourselves. When together we see God's transcendent glory and give ourselves to His call for the earth to be filled with the radiance of who He is, we will be united as never before. We will proclaim Christ in our preaching and in our relationships. Every small thing that has separated us will fall away and the world will know that Jesus is the Son of God.

GOD'S PURPOSE: THE WORSHIP OF THE NATIONS

The acts of the Holy Spirit that brought the gospel to the nations culminates in the book of Revelation, before the throne of God. The Apostle John records this vision of worship and also reveals why God designed missions as He has:

> And they sang a new song, saying, "Worthy are you to take the scroll and to open its seals, for you were slain, and by your blood you ransomed people for God from every tribe and language and people and nation, and you have made them a kingdom and priests to our God, and they shall reign on the earth." (Revelation 5:9-10)

We are moved by the Holy Spirit to go to the nations, to people groups who have not yet heard, because God is using us to prepare for that great day. In his book, *Let the Nations be Glad*, John Piper tells us something of the design of this Scripture:

> The missionary vision behind this scene is that the task of the church is *to gather the ransomed from all peoples, tongues, tribes and nations.* All peoples must be reached because God has appointed people to believe the gospel that He has ransomed through the death of His Son. The design of the atonement prescribes the design of mission strategy. And the design of the atonement (Christ's ran-

som, verse 9) is *universal* in the sense that it extends to all peoples and *definite* in that it effectually ransoms some from each of those peoples. Therefore the missionary task is to gather the ransomed from all the peoples through preaching the gospel.[7]

Someday we will stand before God's glorious throne, joined by those from every tribe and tongue and people and nation, and by myriads of angels who have watched in amazement across the ages as Jesus has been building His Church. The worship that we will share will be in celebration of our great God and His triumph in the Son of His glory. Every time we pray, serve and give toward the fulfillment of His Kingdom, God is preparing us for The Day of the Lord.

GROUP STUDY GUIDE AND PERSONAL APPLICATION

1. It has been almost 2,000 years since Jesus promised to return. In the eyes of this world, He is very slow in keeping that promise. God says He is not slow, He is patient. What is the difference?

2. In your own words, describe why God is patient. What does that patience mean for your loved ones who do not know Him?

3. What does it mean that Jesus did not come as a means of condemnation, but as a means of redemption? Why are people condemned?

4. When you think of how Jesus turned the hearts of His disciples from the kingdom of this world to His eternal Kingdom, what

[7]John Piper, *Let the Nations Be Glad*, (Grand Rapids, MI: Baker Books, 1993), p. 197.

implications do you see for your own life or for the life of your church?

5. As you think of the acts of the Holy Spirit in the building of the first century Church, what is it that amazes you the most? How can our churches look more like the churches we study there?

6. Do you really believe that political systems are irrelevant? What system of government do you feel creates the best environment for church growth?

7. How can God use someone as evil as Pharaoh or Nero to fulfill His will? Has God been limited by rebellious men and women in the building of His Church?

8. How do you think mission strategies need to change in order for us to bring the gospel to nations and people groups, in order to prepare for the day pictured for us in Revelation 5:9-10?

REFLECTIONS, COMMITMENTS AND PRAYER

Has God given you His heart for His world? Have you desired more of a passion for missions than you have experienced? Ask God to give you His heart, and to show you how to walk with Him in the building of His Church around the world. Pray that God would show you how your church might become more like the churches we read about in the book of Acts. Worship God for His sovereignty in the building of His Church and ask Him to use you in filling the earth with His glory.

The kingdom of heaven is like treasure hidden in a field, which a man found and covered up. Then in his joy he goes and sells all that he has and buys that field.

Matthew 13:44

4

The Joy of the Harvest

We have seen that God is building a Kingdom that will last forever and that His glory is seen in His triumph over His enemies. In the Great Commission, the Lord Jesus is not only inviting His disciples who stood with Him on the day of His ascension into the process with Him as He is building His Church, but He is inviting you and me as well. When God gives us a heart for Him and for His Kingdom, He will use us just as He did the very ordinary disciples of His own Son.

When we read the book of Acts, our hearts are thrilled with the incredible works of the Holy Spirit as the New Testament Church is born and begins to grow by God's grace. We are in awe of how God takes ordinary people and does extraordinary things through them. We hunger to be used of God like that and to see Him continue to build His Church by the work of His Spirit through us.

What qualified the first disciples of the Lord to be used like that? Only one thing: God placed His hand on them and made them His own. He called them and filled them. It was God who equipped them by His Spirit to do His work. They brought an openness, a willingness to be used of Him, and a heart of obedience. God took them from that place and put His glory on display through them in the building of His Church.

As we study the first thirteen chapters of Acts, we do not see the apostles and disciples dreaming and then coming with their visions for how the Great Commission might be accomplished. God was always so far ahead of them! He was leading and they were following with responsive hearts. This gives me great hope in the ministry because I am so slow to learn.

One of the most valuable lessons that I have learned by God's grace is that it is not my responsibility to figure out what God wants me to do. He carries the responsibility to show me what He wants me to do. If the pressure was on me to "find God's will" or "discern His leading," I believe I would miss it most of the time because I am made out of dust. Fortunately, God has given me His Word and His Spirit, and He is quite capable of showing me what He wants me to do as I serve Him. My responsibility is to come with a responsive heart and to listen to the voice of my Shepherd.

When God gives us a heart for Him and His Kingdom, He will begin to do His acts through us by His Spirit just as He did in the Early Church. He will orient our hearts around missions. He will transform our churches and orient our resources around the Great Commission. God will then invite us to join Him in His harvest.

THE HARVEST IS AT THE END OF THE AGE

In Matthew 13, Jesus taught His disciples a parable about weeds sown in a field of wheat. The disciples did not understand the parable, so they asked the Lord to explain it to them. In response,

Jesus gave a graphic description of the process and the battles in preparation for the harvest. We might be surprised where we fit in as we look at the picture:

> He answered, "The one who sows the good seed is the Son of Man. The field is the world, and the good seed is the children of the kingdom. The weeds are the sons of the evil one, and the enemy who sowed them is the devil. The harvest is the close of the age, and the reapers are angels. (Matthew 13:37-39)

We are not the ones doing the harvesting. God's angels are. Jesus is the One who sowed the seed. But there is an enemy who sowed weeds in the midst of the good seed, the wheat. That enemy is the devil who lives to destroy the harvest. The hope of the harvest is in the hands of our sovereign God:

> Just as the weeds are gathered and burned with fire, so will it be at the close of the age. The Son of Man will send his angels, and they will gather out of his kingdom all causes of sin and all law-breakers, (Matthew 13:40-41)

At the end of the age, when the harvest takes place, Jesus the Son of Man will send His angels out to the field, and they will begin the harvest. Those who love sin and do evil will be weeded out of His Kingdom, and they will be burned in the fire:

> and throw them into the fiery furnace. In that place there will be weeping and gnashing of teeth. Then the righteous will shine like the sun in the kingdom of their Father. He who has ears, let him hear. (Matthew 13:42-43)

The angels of God will throw the evil ones out of the Kingdom and into the fiery furnace. In that place there is only weeping, hatred, bitterness and anger. Now that the Kingdom has been freed from the weeds and cleansed from evil, the children of the Kingdom—the righteous ones—will shine like the sun. We must heed the warning: "he who has ears, let him hear." If God has given us by His Spirit the gift of ears to hear Him, we are stewards of that grace. This is a call for us who have placed our faith in Christ to live in holiness and obedience as citizens of His Kingdom.

THE FIELDS ARE READY NOW

After Jesus ministered to the woman at the well in John chapter four, He talked to the disciples about the harvest. His disciples had brought food to share with Him, but He responded:

> Meanwhile the disciples were urging him, saying, "Rabbi, eat." But he said to them, "I have food to eat that you do not know about." (John 4:31-32)

The Son of God was sustained by a Life Source that the disciples did not understand at this point in their walk with the Lord:

> So the disciples said to one another, "Has anyone brought him something to eat?" Jesus said to them, "My food is to do the will of him who sent me and to accomplish his work." (John 4:33-34)

The disciples did not grasp the reality of Jesus' relationship with His Father. He was filled up and satisfied in doing the Father's will. Then Jesus told them what the Father's work was all about:

> Do you not say, "There are yet four months, then comes the harvest'? Look, I tell you, lift up your eyes, and see that the fields are white for harvest." (John 4:35)

As the disciples looked out to the fields, according to the timetable of their calendar, the harvest was not yet ready. "Look," Jesus said. "The fields are ready now!" The harvest is on the Father's timetable, and when He says the field is ready, it is time for the harvest to begin. How often we feel that those around us are not ready, nor are we. The Lord of the harvest is calling us to join Him now:

> Already the one who reaps is receiving wages and gathering fruit for eternal life, so that sower and reaper may rejoice together. For here the saying holds true, "One sows and another reaps." (John 4:36-37)

In this Scripture, God calls us to join Him in the reaping. As we share with Him in the harvest, we also share with Him in His joy. Isn't it wonderful that our Father promises us "wages" as we join His harvest workers? Just as Jesus was satisfied and filled up in doing His Father's will, our satisfaction and joy will overflow in serving Him:

> I sent you to reap that for which you did not labor. Others have labored, and you have entered into their labor. (John 4:38)

For those of us who serve the Lord, this verse touches our hearts deeply. We know too well the truth that Jesus sets before His disciples. Others have gone before us and have done the hard work. When we think of the choice servants of the Lord, who have laid down their lives over the centuries for the Kingdom, we feel our unworthiness to follow in their train.

God's servants today might spend long hours on airplanes but can still get anywhere in this world in a relatively short time. Just a few short years ago, it would probably take many difficult months to make the same journey. Today we might be separated from our families for weeks, but in generations past, others were willing to serve alone for years. Sometimes we get sick from food that we are unaccustomed to eating, but over the centuries many of our Lord's servants endured months and even years of severe illness to persevere in the Father's call. We may become depressed and worn down in the battles of ministry, but countless heroes carried their own coffins with them when they went to the field. Others have done the hard work, and we have the joy of joining them and the Lord of the harvest in preparing for the end of the age.

THE CHURCH IS THE CENTER FOR MISSIONS

As we think about our Father's invitation to join Him in the harvest, what are some things we might do in order to serve more effectively?

In order for us to mobilize our people and orient their hearts around what God is doing, we need a much bigger view of His Church. We must see the Church as the center of His heart, His purposes and His strategy. Too often we have given the task of mobilizing God's people for missions over to mission agencies, and we have seen local churches as a support base for what the agencies are doing.

In their very challenging book, *Changing the Mind of Missions*, James F. Engle and William A. Dyrness put it this way:

> A central theological reality is that the church is uniquely equipped to be the locus of missions because it is essentially missionary by its very nature. This means that the church itself is the missionary reality that God sends into the world—it is far more than an institutional source from which funds and missionaries are sent or agency-developed programs carried out. Indeed it is both the message and the medium expressing the fullness of the reign of Christ.[8]

We thank God for mission agencies. I love them! One of my great joys in ministry is going to a mission center to bring the en-

[8]James F. Engle and William A. Dyrness, *Changing the Mind of Missions* (Downers Grove, IL: InterVarsity Press, 2000), p. 74.

couragement of the Scriptures to brothers and sisters there. I am continually amazed and challenged by the depth of maturity and godliness that I see among missionaries. I have met some of the highest quality, most competent and deeply committed people I have ever known on the mission field. Where would the Church and missions be without these choice servants and bold agencies?

The first and second great waves of missions since the Early Church took place in the nineteenth and twentieth centuries. Thousands of missionaries were mobilized by mission agencies in Europe and North America. Unfortunately, sometimes in this process, the local church has been seen as little more than a source for candidates and funds which enable the mission agencies and parachurch organizations to continue their great work of fulfilling the Great Commission.

The focus of missions needs to shift back to the local church. Mission agencies and parachurch organizations still have their places and can provide a strong support to churches in mobilizing and strategizing. But overall authority, shepherding, prayer, and vision for both the people involved and the task before us must return to the local church. We need a stronger, more strategic alliance between mission agencies and churches.

Churches must be more proactive in sending out young people to the field, putting them in an environment where God might place a call in their hearts to give their lives to missions. Missions and elder boards hold the primary responsibility for evaluating the call, giftedness, character, and maturity of potential missionaries. Elders must continue to shepherd their people on the field.

How do we do that? I am not sure, but seeking God for wisdom and direction in the process, and asking Him to show the way would be a good place to start. Perhaps members of the elder board could regularly take trips to visit their people on the field, not primarily to evaluate results but to care for hearts and families.

Projects overseas might be initiated by local churches and then fulfilled by strong involvement on the part of their lay people. These projects might be either short or long term. My brothers and sisters at Sawyer Highlands Baptist Church in Sawyer, Michigan, developed a "sister" relationship with churches in both Romania and Brazil. On a regular basis, they have sent church staff and lay leadership to disciple pastors and leaders in these churches. This ministry, which has gone on for many years now, has brought incredible fruit and lasting relationships of mutual strengthening and encouragement.

One of the best places to begin in missions outreach like this is to simply pray that God would show you what He is doing around the world and then ask how you can be a part of His great work. This time on your knees as church and mission leaders can be the most fruitful aspect of the entire process. In fact, God's great church-building enterprise began in the first place with one hundred and twenty brothers and sisters on their faces before the Lord for a period of ten days. You can read about that in Acts chapter one. God moved from that upper room around the world in a way that they never envisioned nor had the courage or planning skills to devise.

THE COMMISSION IS TO MAKE DISCIPLES

As we look at God's work of building His Church around the world, we stand in amazement before Him. We worship when we see how our sovereign Lord has glorified Himself in fulfilling His will, bringing to Himself those whom He has called to salvation. The work of evangelism in these last several years is incredible in its fruitfulness. The numbers of people being saved and the rate of church growth in Asia, Latin America and Africa is almost beyond comprehension. This rapid growth comes at a cost. When I am teaching in these areas or our staff has the opportunity to serve in these places, we often hear that "the church here is a mile wide and an inch deep." Look with me at the Great Commission once again:

> And Jesus came and said to them, "All authority in heaven and on earth has been given to me. Go therefore and make disciples of all nations, baptizing them in the name of the Father and of the Son and of the Holy Spirit, teaching them to observe all that I have commanded you. And behold, I am with you always, to the end of the age." (Matthew 28:18-20)

The primary command is to "make disciples" of all nations. God gave us the task of *discipling* the nations! This is an area where we in the developed nations can be a substantial resource for the emerging churches in the developing nations. God has gifted these churches with incredible evangelists, and countless thousands are coming to Christ. What is needed in these churches are helps with discipleship and leadership development.

God has gifted many of us in the developed nations with training and experience in these areas. For us to stand alongside our brothers and sisters in the emerging Church, as partners in the ministry, bringing the resources and materials God has given us the grace to develop, can be a source of great help and encouragement to them. In our own experience, the "Pastors Training Workshops" that we have been able to take to Latin America and Asia have been wonderfully fruitful in this very ministry.*

---

*For more information on our pastors' training workshops, contact the Director of our International Ministries, Craig Parro, at cparro@leadershipresources.org.

For us in the developed nations to walk with God in the building of His Church around the world, we need a shift in focus. If we would be effective in discipling the nations, evangelism cannot be our only objective. Evangelism is done far more effectively through relationships within one's own culture, and to send expensive missionaries from far off places to do evangelism lessens both the effectiveness and the efficiency of the ministries. We need to focus our resources of finances, gifts and time into the ministries of discipleship and leadership development where a healthy, reproducing church already exists.

BUILDING STRATEGIC PARTNERSHIPS

One of the ways we can focus our resources more effectively is in the building of strategic partnerships. The nature of missions is somewhat like the nature of the Church. In the Body of Christ, no one possesses all of the gifts and abilities needed for the building up of the church. God sovereignly blesses each member of the body with unique gifts in order for the church to function according to His design. That is often the way it is in missions and in the church at large. God entrusts a variety of resources and abilities, and often a unique focus, to local churches and mission agencies.

The time is short, and the opportunities are great. We cannot afford to squander resources of people, money and time by always "going it alone" in the work of missions. We can work far more effectively and efficiently by partnering with one another.

We love partnerships in Leadership Resources. Our longest and most fruitful partnership has been with World Radio Missionary Fellowship (HCJB) in Quito, Ecuador. Our shared ministry is called APOYO ("helps" in Spanish). For years, we have shared staff, funds and facilities in order to conduct "Pastor's Training Workshops" throughout Latin America. We have shared both the burdens of the work and the joy of the harvest with our beloved brothers and sisters at HCJB.

We have also enjoyed partnering with the Billy Graham Evangelistic Association, South American Mission, SIM (formerly known as Sudan Interior Mission), Wycliffe Bible Translators and the Baptist General Conference. In China we have joined in the work with Christian Communications Limited and Partners International.

Let me tell you about a particularly exciting partnership we have enjoyed over the past few years. Some time ago I was invited to Peru to encourage the staffs of Wycliffe Bible Translators and South American Mission. This is a regular part of my ministry. I invited the chairman of our board, Jeff Lampos, to accompany me on this trip. Américo Saavedra, the director of APOYO, was born in the city of Pucallpa in Peru where these ministries would take place. He was also there during that time for other ministry responsibilities.

While we were in Pucallpa, in addition to the two mission agencies where I was invited to teach, we spent time with a number of other missions. Each of them shared with us the need for leadership development and asked if we could help. On the first Sunday we were there, we had worshiped at the central evangelical church in Pucallpa. During the service, the pastor had talked about a boat they wanted to purchase, and they received an offering for that project.

A couple of days later, Americo told us that the mission committee of the church would like to meet with us and take us on a boat ride. As Jeff, Américo and I sat with the brothers and sisters from the mission committee, they shared a dream with us. Pucallpa is located in the eastern jungle of Peru on the Ucayali River. This is a huge river system, as it is the main tributary of the Amazon as it flows through Peru. Our friends told us that there are villages all up and down the river, and Pucallpa is strategically located in the very center of these villages.

A few years earlier, the church in Pucallpa had purchased a smaller boat and began going up and down the river to bring the gospel to these villages. Many people in these small towns placed their faith in Christ. The brothers and sisters in Pucallpa then began to help organize churches around the new believers. They knew that leaders needed to be trained, so they started taking more and more trips up and down the Ucayali River to train these leaders. But now there were far too many churches and leaders for them to train alone, and they wanted to know if we would help them.

What kind of help did they need? I think that Jeff and I both expected them to ask us for money, but they never did that. They asked if we would send our team of teachers to help them in their ministry of leadership development. They would do the organizational work and help the pastors get there if we could provide a library of study resources and training in preaching and teaching from the Scriptures.

Later, Jeff told me that he had spent the entire time during the meeting looking down at his shoes and saying to himself, "This is what they are doing with what God has given to them. What are we doing with what God has given to us?"

We were delighted to share as partners with our brothers and sisters in Pucallpa. In fact, we have had several workshops in that great city. Just a few months ago, we conducted a workshop with three hundred pastors and saw God do a beautiful work of healing among the fractional groups that had developed among them. That is the fruit of sharing together in the harvest, and walking together as partners.

RELEASING OUR RESOURCES

When we look at what we can bring to God's great mission enterprise today, we must look at our money. That is one of the primary resources He entrusted to us in the developed nations for the building of His Church around the world.

I have been in many places in the world where pastors work full time at a business or on a farm and pastor three churches at the same time. Their work enables them to earn three dollars a day or less to care for their families. But these wonderful servants are joyfully laying down their lives to serve the Lord and His Church. In fact, they would look at this lifestyle as no sacrifice at all.

I am not arguing here for us to provide for their salaries as that is the responsibility of their churches. In the long run, we don't help them if they develop a dependence upon outside funding in this area. God would have our brothers and sisters in these churches learn to trust Him in faith and to sacrificially give in order to provide for their pastors and elders. What we can provide is funding for facilities and for ministry resources.

A love for material things has stolen away a vision for missions among affluent nations. In fact, for many, the seemingly insatiable appetite for possessions and the relentless pursuit of financial security has stolen away one of God's most gracious gifts—a spirit of contentment. This appetite has also been used by our enemy to develop a spiritual stronghold of slavery in which he keeps many of God's people from going to the field or giving to others who go. Credit card debt and other liabilities which flow from our inability to discern our wants from our needs places too many of us in such bondage that if God called us to a new level of commitment to missions, we could hardly respond. Going to the field would be almost out of the question and increased giving nearly impossible.

Jesus addressed this very issue as He taught His disciples about "kingdom seeking" in the book of Luke. As our Lord teaches, a man who has a problem with his brother over a family inheritance interrupts him:

> Someone in the crowd said to him, "Teacher, tell my brother to divide the inheritance with me." But he said to him, "Man, who made me a judge or arbitrator over you?" (Luke 12:13-14)

Jesus immediately sees right through this man's motives. Rather than taking his side and pursuing "justice," Christ confronts the disciples and those gathered with them about greed and materialism:

> And he said to them, "Take care, and be on your guard against all covetousness, for one's life does not consist in the abundance of his possessions." (Luke 12:15)

Have we ever seen a clearer definition of materialism than what the Lord Jesus sets before us here—a person whose life consists of their possessions? From the beginning to the end, filling every moment, every desire, every space of life is the pursuit of things. Jesus follows His confrontation with a story:

> And he told them a parable, saying, "The land of a rich man produced plentifully, and he thought to himself, 'What shall I do, for I have nowhere to store my crops?'" (Luke 12:16-17)

This man is facing a horrible problem. His land is so productive that he does not have enough room to store all of the stuff that his life is producing. His search for the solution takes place only within the confines of his own heart and mind. He does not pray, nor seek the counsel of his elders. He only reasons with himself:

And he said, "I will do this: I will tear down my barns and build larger ones, and there I will store all my grain and my goods." (Luke 12:18)

The more this man thinks about the horrendous problem he is facing—the more he considers how to care for all of the stuff of his life—the more he realizes what he should do. He needs to tear down his barns! They are far too small. What he thinks he needs is more barns, bigger barns:

And I will say to my soul, "Soul, you have ample goods laid up for many years; relax, eat, drink, be merry." (Luke 12:19)

When all of this poor man's bigger barns are filled with the stuff of his life, he can stand back, glorying in all that he accomplished and produced. At last he can lay back and take life easy. He concludes that he can never live long enough to spend all of the things he accumulated:

But God said to him, "Fool! This night your soul is required of you, and the things you have prepared, whose will they be?" (Luke 12:20)

There is one thing this man has not considered. There is a God to whom he owes an account of his life. That very night God commands that his life be taken and that he should stand before the judgment throne. All of the accumulated stuff of this man's life will now be enjoyed by someone else:

So is the one who lays up treasure for himself and is not rich toward God. (Luke 12:21)

We never see a person who gives himself to the pursuit of things in this life actually come to the place where he can enjoy all that is accumulated. One of two things happens. Either he is taken from this life before he can enjoy his stuff, or right up to the very end of his life he is still giving himself to the accumulation of things because that is all his heart has ever learned to do.

God does not call us to accumulate things in this world. He calls us to be "rich toward Him." He desires our hearts to be filled to overflowing with the treasures of knowing Him and the joys of serving Him.

THE FREEDOM TO BE KINGDOM SEEKERS

After the parable of the "rich fool," Jesus teaches His disciples how their Father has set them free from the pursuit of things. We can live a life free from worry and the anxiety that demands we accumulate more by trusting in the God who promises to provide for us:

> And he said to his disciples, "Therefore I tell you, do not be anxious about your life, what you will eat, nor about your body, what you will put on. For life is more than food, and the body more than clothing." (Luke 12:22-23)

Life consists of more than what we eat and what we wear. Jesus is turning the hearts of His disciples toward eternal things. He then uses the birds as an illustration of how He desires us to live—free from cares and pressures—because we know that He will provide:

> Consider the ravens: they neither sow nor reap, they have neither storehouse nor barn, and yet God feeds them. Of how much more value are you than the birds! (Luke 12:24)

How wonderful it is to see ourselves through God's eyes. We are valuable to Him, more valuable than the birds that He cares for day after day. If we trust in Him as the birds do, how will that change the way we live in this world? We will live free from worry and free to serve Him:

And which of you by being anxious can add a single hour to his span of life? If then you are not able to do as small a thing as that, why are you anxious about the rest? (Luke 12:25-26)

God is sovereign over the times of our lives. No matter how much we worry, we cannot add even one hour to the span of our days. What makes us think that by our anxieties we can change anything else about our lives or our circumstances?

Consider the lilies, how they grow: they neither toil nor spin, yet I tell you, even Solomon in all his glory was not arrayed like one of these. But if God so clothes the grass, which is alive in the field today, and tomorrow is thrown into the oven, how much more will he clothe you, O you of little faith! (Luke 12:27-28)

Jesus talks about the flowers of the field just as He did the birds of the air. Here we find the promise that our Father will clothe us just as He promises to feed us. In light of the Father's promises, the Lord Jesus calls His disciples to focus their hearts on what is eternal:

And do not seek what you are to eat and what you are to drink, nor be worried. For all the nations of the world seek after these things, and your Father knows that you need them. (Luke 12:29-30)

The focus of our hearts will determine the direction and pursuits of our lives. The world runs after the things that Jesus describes here. We see this so clearly today. The world is running after dollars, oil, gold, food and the fleeting security they bring. But we have a Father that knows we need these things, and He promises to provide them for us:

Instead, seek his kingdom, and these things will be added to you. (Luke 12:31)

In light of our Father's eternal commitments to us as His children and His promises to care for every need of our lives, He calls us to seek His Kingdom. In these truths we find one of our greatest secrets for contentment. Our Heavenly Father knows that we are living in a physical world with real needs to be met in order to maintain our lives here. We can seek Him and His Kingdom with a whole heart and, at the same time, be completely confident and free that our Father will provide everything we need along the way.

PURSES THAT CAN HOLD TREASURES

After teaching His disciples about "kingdom seeking," Jesus makes this incredible statement to them:

> Fear not, little flock, for it is your Father's good pleasure to give you the kingdom. (Luke 12:32)

How does our Father set us free from the pursuit of things? He gives us His Kingdom as an inheritance in His Son! We already have it all; we do not need to spend our lives accumulating things. In light of God's provisions for us and His commitments to our care, this, then, is our Lord's counsel:

> Sell your possessions, and give to the needy. Provide yourselves with moneybags that do not grow old, with a treasure in the heavens that does not fail, where no thief approaches and no moth destroys. (Luke 12:33)

Jesus tells His disciples to give their resources away! Give to the poor. Then He sets before us this fascinating picture. We can make "moneybags that do not grow old!" In this world our purses wear out. They develop holes in them. When we put money in the top, it falls out the bottom. Often we put money aside for a "rainy day" or for something we might need or enjoy in the future, and then one of the children gets sick. The money that we set aside falls out of the bottom of the purse. The car or the furnace break down or the roof leaks. Our purses wear out.

Christ promises that we can carry purses that hold real, lasting treasures by investing in what is eternal: people! Treasures in heaven do not run out; they do not rust; there are no thieves to steal them away. Listen, then, to our Lord's summary statement:

> For where your treasure is, there will your heart be also.
> (Luke 12:34)

Sometimes when we see people in this world building their lives around things, we are tempted to say, "they are doing that because that is where their heart is." That is not what Jesus is teaching us here. He is saying, "that is where your heart will be." He is telling us that the desires of our hearts develop in the direction in which we focus. If we keep focusing on things, our hearts will become more and more consumed with what we desire to consume. Before long we become owned by what we want to own. But if we focus our hearts on what is eternal, God will grip our hearts for eternity.

There are two great turning points awaiting us in our churches in the affluent developed nations, if God would use us increasingly in missions. First of all, we must see that one of the primary roles that He desires us to fill in the developing world is that of funding. He equipped us uniquely to give. Secondly, we must learn to give without maintaining control. If we give freely and trust the leaders in the developing nations to use the funds as God directs them, we will stand amazed at the incredible things God will do through them.

EMPOWERING LEADERS IN THE DEVELOPING WORLD

God has raised up a new generation of leaders in the emerging Church around the world. Many of these leaders are gifted, highly educated and mature. We see them pastoring churches, giving direction to evangelistic campaigns, leading mission agencies, and mentoring other pastors. They are most often skilled communicators and definitely faithful servants.

This new generation of leadership can be trusted with the ministry. Much of missions from the developed world came in the past to these leaders with a paternalistic attitude, from "the top down," to help them in the work. Too often we have come with the attitude that we are the ones who possess the knowledge, experience, techniques, and resources that will enable their ministries to flourish. If they would just follow our counsel and example, they would have the same success we have enjoyed.

What incredible arrogance! Do we want them to have the same success as we have had? In most of their nations, the Church has experienced growth far beyond what we have seen. Unfortunately, too often we did not come to these leaders with the humility of a learner's attitude. Rather than coming as partners in the harvest, we have come as experts. Truthfully, in many of these situations, we have far more to learn from these brothers and sisters than we have to teach them. What God has taught them about prayer, endurance, faithfulness, integrity, and evangelism would be so helpful to us and our churches if we were willing to be taught by them. Attitudes of pride and paternalism have cost us dearly in the work of God's Kingdom.

If God would give us the grace to bring as servants what He has entrusted to us—the funds, the materials for discipleship, the experience in leadership development—and then partner with leaders in the developing nations as brothers and sisters together in His vineyard, we would see amazing fruit. God would be glorified both in our humility and in the way our churches and theirs would flourish through the mutual discipleship we would share.

In our small mission at Leadership Resources International, God has given the director of our international ministries, Craig Parro, great wisdom in this area. He prayed and sought the Lord for His wisdom and leading for staff and for the direction of this work. I am both challenged and encouraged as I see him spend hours in prayer, humbling himself before the Lord. I am amazed at his aggressive faith and the boldness with which he has responded to what God has given him to do.

Over the years I have had the privilege of working with two of the most gifted mission leaders of the developing nations. These are men that Craig chose for his team. Américo Saavedra, born in Peru, South America, is the director of our ministry throughout Latin America. Henry Chua, a Filipino of Chinese descent, is the director of our ministry in China. Both of these men are from developing nations. Never have I met more godly and mature servants of the Lord! Do they need me to tell them how to be effective in ministry? Hardly! I need to learn from them. They are a joy to serve with, and I am grateful for every opportunity to walk alongside them and for them to be my teachers. There are hundreds of other potential leaders like Henry and Américo who we must find, fund and empower.

A KINGDOM LIFESTYLE

When God gives us His heart for His world and orients our desires around the joy of the harvest, we will develop a Kingdom Lifestyle. This new lifestyle will be seen in two areas: our money and our prayers. Since our passions drive us in life, when God grips our passions and desires for Himself and His kingdom He owns everything we are and do. When He owns our money we live to participate in the building of His Church more than we live to build our own security and pleasures. When God owns our prayers, we spend less time asking for what has to do with us, and more time seeking Him for the display of His glory in the building of the Church around the world.

Jesus taught His own disciples about Kingdom praying when He looked upon the multitudes with compassion, knowing that they were helpless, like sheep without a shepherd.

> Then he said to his disciples, "The harvest is plentiful, but the laborers are few; therefore pray earnestly to the Lord of the harvest to send out laborers into his harvest." (Matthew 9:37-38)

The Lord Jesus was opening the eyes of His disciples, enabling them to see people the way He saw them. He was lifting their eyes above themselves to see the glory of the awaiting harvest. Jesus then confronted His followers about their prayer lives. "Ask the Lord of the harvest to send out workers!" I think Jesus confronted them in this way because His disciples were not asking the Father to send out workers. I think they were asking for smaller things.

In my own walk with the Lord, I have seen my need for growth in my prayer life even greater than my need for growth in my attitudes toward money. I love to give, but even after many years of knowing the Lord and even serving Him, I am still confronted with the ugly reality of how many of my prayers are oriented around me, those I love and what I am doing. Perhaps my greatest need as I have grown in the Lord is a reformation and revival in my prayers, away from who I am to who God is, away from what I am doing to what He is doing.

Have you experienced a revival like this? What percentage of your prayers, if God would answer them, would directly benefit you or someone close to you, such as a loved one or a church member? What percentage of your prayers are oriented around the building of the Church around the world? What percentage are for raising up evangelists, pastors and teachers in needy countries, or for churches in hurting places, or for brothers and sisters suffering for their faith?

The nature of the flesh drives us to consume our lives and our resources upon ourselves. When our Father owns the passions of our hearts, He will focus our desires and every resource upon Himself and His glory. That is a Kingdom Lifestyle.

THE TREASURE AND THE PEARL

Jesus taught a parable to His disciples that gave them a picture of how valuable the Kingdom of heaven is in His eyes:

> The kingdom of heaven is like treasure hidden in a field, which a man found and covered up. Then in his joy he goes and sells all that he has and buys that field. (Matthew 13:44)

We, too, can gain a small sense of how precious God's Kingdom is to His heart as we read this parable. There is a treasure hidden in the field. Someone discovers it, amazed at his good fortune. He quickly hides it again and, filled with great joy, sells all that he has and purchases the entire field:

> Again, the kingdom of heaven is like a merchant in search of fine pearls, who, on finding one pearl of great value, went and sold all that he had and bought it. (Matthew 13:45-46)

Our Lord followed with a similar parable. This time the treasure is a fine pearl. A merchant finds one of great value. His response is to sell everything he has in order to buy that pearl. Again, the teaching is about the Kingdom.

Who is the man who finds the treasure in the field? Who is the merchant who discovers the pearl? Who sells everything he owns in order to purchase what he sees as precious? It is God! God is the One who found the treasure and the Merchant who discovered the pearl. These parables are about the Kingdom. We did not purchase the Kingdom; God has done that. He is the One who sold everything He has in order to purchase the treasure and the pearl.

God saw the Church of the Lord Jesus as the most precious treasure in all the world, and He gave all He had, His own precious treasure, His only Son, in order to purchase what was so valuable in His eyes. He gave Himself for you and me and for our brothers and sisters in the Body of Christ throughout the ages.

When God gives us the eyes to see His Church with the same precious value that is in His eyes, we, too, will sell everything we have in order to walk with Him in the purchasing of His Kingdom. He will fill us with the same joy that is His in the building of His Church. God prepares our hearts to meet our Bridegroom as we replace the treasures in our hearts with the treasure of His heart.

GROUP STUDY GUIDE AND PERSONAL APPLICATION

1. How did the comments on "finding God's will" as opposed to God showing us what He desires us to do strike you? What are the implications of this understanding concerning our freedom before the Lord and our involvement in missions?

2. Just like those whom Jesus was teaching in John 4, we might not feel that the "harvest" is ready. What does it mean to us today when we hear the Lord say that the harvest is ripe right now?

3. If the Church is the center for missions, how do you evaluate your own church's involvement in missions and with the missionaries that you send out?

4. In our last chapter, we looked at evangelizing the nations. In the Great Commission, the call is to disciple the nations. What do you think needs to change in our mission programs in order for us to fulfill that call?

5. How do you respond to the thought that one of the greatest resources that we can bring to missions today is money? Does that diminish our stature in the Church around the world?

6. How much do you feel materialism has affected our involvement in missions? Do you feel that your "life consists of your possessions?" Why, or why not?

7. When you look at your own life experiences, how have you seen your "purses wear out" and develop holes in them? How have you seen God use you to invest in heavenly treasures that cannot be exhausted?

8. Is it possible for us to entrust large sums of money to church leaders of developing nations without controlling those funds? Why, or why not?

9. As you study the parables of the treasure and the pearl, what strikes you the most? How do we replace the treasures of our hearts with the treasure of God's heart?

REFLECTIONS, COMMITMENTS AND PRAYER

Have you seen the harvest through the eyes of the Lord Jesus? As you look at your family, your friends and your neighbors, are the fields ready and ripe? Ask God to show you how our battles with materialism have affected your freedom to participate in the harvest. Pray that He will show you and your church how to walk with Him in missions today in order to effectively build His Kingdom. Ask Him to replace the treasures of your heart with the treasure of His heart.

Since all these things are thus to be dissolved, what sort of people ought you to be in lives of holiness and godliness, waiting for and hastening the coming of the day of God.

2 Peter 3:11-12a

5

A Hunger for Holiness

Peter teaches us about God's patience and His heart for everyone to come to repentance. He does not want us to perish; He is waiting to send His Son in The Day of the Lord so that many more might respond to the gospel of Christ and be saved. God is putting off the terror and the glory of that Day while He is building the Church of the Lord Jesus.

Earlier in the chapter, Peter talked about the "scoffers" who asked, "Where is this coming He promised?" The scoffers lived as if nothing would change because, in their eyes nothing had changed for so long. The Scriptures talk about the return of Christ. But it has been two millennia now, and He has not come back to rule. Today's scoffers are oblivious to the works of God as He is building His Church and fulfilling His will in this world; their eyes are blinded to how God is preparing to fill the earth with His glory.

Jesus will return in His glory at a time set by the Father and at a time that the scoffers do not expect. He will come at a time when many believers do not expect His return. His appearance will be a surprise to them, like a thief coming in the night:

> But the day of the Lord will come like a thief. The heavens will disappear with a roar; the elements will be destroyed by fire, and the earth and everything in it will be laid bare. (2 Peter 3:10)

When we least expect our lives to change, Jesus will return. Like a thief invading our privacy and violating what we protect, Christ will invade time and space. He will come to this world that He made and fulfill every purpose for its creation and every promise of history. This time our Lord will not come as a baby with His incarnation recognized by a chorus of angels and a few shepherds. Rather, Jesus will come with all of the power and glory that belongs to the Lion of Judah and the heavens will disappear.

THE ROAR OF THE LION

The heavens will disappear! That thought is so far beyond our comprehension. When we look up to the skies now, we have great security, knowing that we will see the clouds, the sun, the moon, the stars, and the planets. As we look to the heavens, we find a sense of security in knowing that this great universe is in place, and we are surrounded with the entire vast array of this creation that has stood for millennia. But it will change. All that we have seen every day of our lives will no longer be there. What people have seen every day since creation will disappear. The heavens will be gone. With a roar unlike any heard in all the realms of time, the glory and security of the heavens will be removed.

The Lord's return will not only consume the heavens; the elements will be destroyed as well. The most basic stuff of the universe will be done away with. Peter comes back to this thought a couple of verses later. He wants us to know the complete and devastating destruction this world will undergo:

...the heavens will be set on fire and dissolved, and the heavenly bodies will melt as they burn! (2 Peter 3:12b)

When Peter talks about destruction on this level with fire and the "elements melting in the heat," we cannot escape thinking about a nuclear holocaust. Might God use the weapons that man has developed to destroy this earth? We do not know, of course, how devastating our nuclear weapons will become in the years ahead or how much darker the heart of mankind will become either. We do know that even now these weapons are capable of such mass destruction that it is beyond our comprehension. I think it is possible that God might use the tools of hatred and death that we have created in His process of destroying the heavens and consuming the elements, but it is hard to believe that we could develop anything powerful enough to cause the heavens to disappear.

I believe that what Peter is describing here in the destruction of our present heavens and earth has to do with the sustaining power of Jesus Christ. The Apostle Paul gave us one of the most beautiful worship songs of the Scriptures in Colossians chapter one. As he lifted Jesus high, exalting Him in His glory and splendor, he said "in Him all things hold together" (Col. 1:17). Jesus is the glue in the universe! He binds the planets in their orbits and holds the atoms and molecules together. In the Father's sovereign timing, our Lord will lift His sustaining hand off of this creation, and in a moment it will all be consumed and disappear.

J.N.D. Kelly, in his commentary of Peter's epistles, talks about these things in this way:

> When the day comes it will be accompanied by a cosmic catastrophe which, the readers are expected to infer, will engulf evildoers like the false teachers. The sketch of the dissolution of the universe by fire is filled out with colorful details and destruction in the

heavens which finds parallels in Old Testament prophecy.[9]

Kelly gives reference to Old Testament prophecy. The prophets foretold The Day of the Lord many centuries before Christ was even born. Look at how the prophet Joel describes His coming:

> And I will show wonders in the heavens and on the earth, blood and fire and columns of smoke. The sun shall be turned to darkness, and the moon to blood, before the great and awesome day of the LORD comes. (Joel 2:30-31)

Joel refers to "wonders in the heavens" and talks about the same fire that Peter describes. He pictures The Day of the Lord as "dreadful." But for those who place their faith in Christ, there is hope:

> And it shall come to pass that everyone who calls on the name of the LORD shall be saved. For in Mount Zion and in Jerusalem there shall be those who escape, as the LORD has said, and among the survivors shall be those whom the LORD calls. (Joel 2:32)

People can be saved simply by "calling on the name of the Lord!" There is deliverance in Him; there is a way to survive the coming holocaust. Our hope is in the name of our God. Later in Joel's prophecy, he returns to his teaching on the Day of the Lord:

> Multitudes, multitudes, in the valley of decision! For the day of the LORD is near in the valley of decision. The sun and the moon are darkened, and the stars withdraw their shining. (Joel 3:14-15)

Joel pictures multitudes in the "valley of decision." As The Day of the Lord draws near, people are confronted more and

---

[9]J.N.D. Kelly, *A Commentary on the Epistles of Peter and Jude*, (New York: Harper & Row Publishers, 1969), p. 363-364.

more with whether they will call upon the Lord in repentance or whether they will remain in their sins. Joel talks about the heavens changing, just as Peter did, and then, also, like Peter, he describes the Lord coming with a "roar:"

> The LORD roars from Zion, and utters his voice from Jerusalem, and the heavens and the earth quake. But the LORD is a refuge to his people, a stronghold to the people of Israel. (Joel 3:16)

Isn't it amazing that in both references in Joel the prophet points us to the hope of God in the midst of the terrible Day of the Lord? First he tells us that those who call on the Lord will be saved, and now he reminds us that the Lord will be a refuge for His people in the midst of the destruction. He is the only stronghold for us when everything around us is changing and when those things which have provided security disappear.

EVERYTHING WILL BE LAID BARE

When Peter describes the terrible devastation of the heavens and the melting of the elements, he does not tell us here that the earth will be destroyed. He says that it will be "exposed." Now, Peter does go on to say, "the heavens will be dissolved" (2 Pet. 3:10,12), but this thought of the earth being laid bare is significant for us to ponder.

When we think back to the effects of the fall and Adam and Eve's first responses to their sin in the environment of their death, we see them hiding (Gen. 3:7). The loin coverings that they made were a means of hiding from one another. Before their sin, they were "naked and unashamed," but now they were naked and ashamed. Where they once had freedom to be seen and known and confidence that they would be accepted, now they lived in fear of being known and rejected.

Then we see God coming into the garden asking, "Adam, where are you" (Gen. 3:8)? Of course, we know that God already knew where Adam was, but Adam did not know where Adam was. He was acting according to his fallen nature, and hiding from God, just as he had done with Eve. The guilt, fear and shame that resulted from his sin caused Adam to withdraw from God and cover himself:

> And he said, "I heard the sound of you in the garden, and I was afraid, because I was naked, and I hid myself." (Genesis 3:10)

From the sin of Adam and Eve came our compulsion to "cover ourselves." The desire to hide is a direct result of the fall. We have come to find our security in revealing to God and others only what we are confident will be accepted and affirmed. On the other hand, we cover what we fear will be rejected. God sent His Son, Jesus, to take our sin and our guilt, our fear and our shame at the cross. That plan of redemption began in the very place where Adam and Eve fell in their rebellion and disobedience, in the Garden of Eden. God's first promise of the Redeemer came as He sought not only Adam and Eve but also you and me in that very same garden:

> I will put enmity between you and the woman, and between your offspring and her offspring; he shall bruise your head, and you shall bruise his heel. (Genesis 3:15)

The head of our great enemy was crushed at the cross of Calvary. Satan "bruised the heel" of our Lord in the pain of His suffering, but the devil was defeated, and God's great eternal plan of redemption was fulfilled in His Son. In God's redemption, we not only receive the forgiveness of our sins but the freedom to know God and to share life intimately with Him and with one another. No longer are we "naked and ashamed," restrained in life by the fear of being known and the need to cover ourselves. Now we have the freedom to know and to be known.

When our Lord returns, all that men and women have kept hidden as they responded to the manipulations and fears of our enemy will be exposed. Whatever has been covered up throughout history will be uncovered and revealed. Everything will be laid bare, and all sin and evil will be exposed. The revelation of Christ and the revelation of history in all of its rebellion and evil will be made known, in order that the righteousness of our God might be declared and worshiped.

How then Shall We Live?

In light of the destruction of the heavens and the earth in the great and terrible Day of the Lord, Peter asks the key question of his third chapter and brings us to the central call of God on our lives in light of His Son's soon return:

> Since all these things are thus to be dissolved, what sort of people ought you to be in lives of holiness and godliness, (2 Peter 3:11)

So what kind of people ought we to be? A people consumed with the intricate details of the Lord's return and its timing? Should we be giving our lives to search out the dates and places that set in motion the events of the "end times?" All of these are important, but they are largely speculative. We can know everything that can be humanly known about these things and still our hearts can be completely unprepared for the return of our Lord. The priority that God sets before us, if we would be ready for The Day of the Lord, is so clear in His Word. The preparation is not of our minds but our hearts, and it has nothing to do with speculations about dates and events and everything to do with holiness.

The Day of the Lord!

We ought to live holy and godly lives. That is the call of the Scriptures and the work of the Holy Spirit as He prepares us for the fulfillment of the ages. Holiness and godliness are precious to our Father and rare in comparison to our passion for facts, principles and insights. Our pursuit of endless speculations concerning end times events rather than holiness has cost us greatly as a Church and has left us woefully unprepared for the suffering, endurance, missions, evangelism, and holiness that are at the heart of God's work in us and for us in these last days.

Paul also linked the grace of God to a life of holiness and to The Day of the Lord as he wrote to Titus:

> For the grace of God has appeared, bringing salvation for all people, training us to renounce ungodliness and worldly passions, and to live self-controlled, upright, and godly lives in the present age, (Titus 2:11-12)

How does God bring us to the places where holiness flourishes in our lives? Is it by rigidly confining laws or the manipulation of guilt or fear? No! It is the grace of God—His favor poured upon us through no merit of our own—that teaches us to deny the passions of this world and to hunger for those things that are right in the eyes of our Father:

> waiting for our blessed hope, the appearing of the glory of our great God and Savior Jesus Christ, who gave himself for us to redeem us from all lawlessness and to purify for himself a people for his own possession who are zealous for good works. (Titus 2:13-14)

We are called to live in holiness and obedience while we are waiting for our Lord to return. This is the "blessed hope" of our lives and of all those who have placed their faith in Him throughout the ages. He gave His own life to redeem us and to prepare us as a holy people for His own possession. While we are waiting for

Him to come back for us, we live with a desire to please Him, eager to do what is right and good.

What do the Scriptures mean when they call us to holiness and godliness? How do we prepare to meet our Bridegroom by living a "holy" life?

WHOLLY OTHER

We often have a narrow understanding of "holiness," limiting the concept to the purity of our lives. Though purity is surely a major focus of holiness in the Scriptures, it is not the heart of its meaning. The central meaning of holiness flows out of the character and nature of God. He is in every way "other" than all that we are.

When God called Isaiah to the ministry as a prophet, He gave Isaiah a vision of His throne in the heavenlies. The scene around God's throne reveals the nature of His holiness. He is lifted high; He is above all that surrounds Him; His glory overwhelms His dwelling places:

> In the year that King Uzziah died I saw the Lord sitting upon a throne, high and lifted up; and the train of his robe filled the temple. (Isaiah 6:1)

The responses of the angels who surround God's throne reflect what the Father desires from our hearts as well. They cover themselves in His presence. They cover their feet and their faces. Unlike Adam and Eve who covered themselves because of their sin, the angels cover themselves because of their unworthiness:

> Above him stood the seraphim. Each had six wings: with two he covered his face, and with two he covered his feet, and with two he flew. (Isaiah 6:2)

What is it about God that causes the angels to see themselves as unworthy? The holiness of God! Continually in His presence, the angels cry out "Holy," and "Glory":

> And one called to another and said: "Holy, holy, holy is the LORD of hosts; the whole earth is full of his glory!" (Isaiah 6:3)

A threefold proclamation of the central attribute of God is the song of the angels that surround His throne. Captivated by the epitome of His Person, the eternal servants of the living God are in awe before Him. They cry out again and again, "Holy, Holy, Holy." They not only recognize the purity of His Person, but they live with the awareness that God is above, He is highly lifted up, He is in every way everything that they are not. He is holy. By His Person and His nature, His glory and His attributes, God is "other" than what the angels are and what we are. This is holiness.

When we become holy we, too, become "other" than everything and everyone else around us. Paul talked to the church at Philippi about this amazing truth.

> Do all things without grumbling or questioning, that you may be blameless and innocent, children of God without blemish in the midst of a crooked and twisted generation, among whom you shine as lights in the world, holding fast to the word of life, so that in the day of Christ I may be proud that I did not run in vain or labor in vain. (Philippians 2:14-16)

Because the Holy Spirit has transformed us and Christ is living within us, our attitudes, priorities and passions are so different than those around us in this world that we appear to them as lights in the darkness. We express the heart of our Lord in a system that is corrupt and depraved. We are unique. We are holy.

HE IS PURE

When Isaiah saw the holiness of God in the vision of His glorious throne and the worship of the angels, he saw his own sin as well. As he experienced the shaking of the doorposts and the threshold of the temple, he said:

> And I said: "Woe is me! For I am lost; for I am a man of unclean lips, and I dwell in the midst of a people of unclean lips; for my eyes have seen the King, the LORD of hosts!" (Isaiah 6:5)

Isaiah saw God's holiness, and then he saw his sin. He was overwhelmed first of all with the knowledge of God's nature as "wholly other" and the purity of His Person, and then Isaiah was overwhelmed with the knowledge of his own sin. He felt "ruined," undone and hopeless in the face of God's holiness. Like Isaiah, we cannot see our sin without seeing the holiness of God first. Only when we see how clean He is do we see how dirty and guilty we are.

In the face of Isaiah's hopelessness, God came to Him. The only One, who in Himself is pure, touched Isaiah and made him pure as well. God took away Isaiah's guilt and atoned for his sin:

> Then one of the seraphim flew to me, having in his hand a burning coal that he had taken with tongs from the altar. And he touched my mouth and said: "Behold, this has touched your lips; your guilt is taken away, and your sin atoned for." (Isaiah 6:6-7)

Do we find this hope in God as well? When we see His holiness and then we see our sin, is there hope that we, too, can be cleansed? The cross is all of our hope! At Calvary, the blood of Jesus washed away our sin and enabled us to stand before a holy God, righteous in His eyes. That was the message of the Apostle Paul to the church at Corinth:

> For our sake he made him to be sin who knew no sin, so that in him we might become the righteousness of God. (2 Corinthians 5:21)

Paul affirmed the church at Colossae with this same message as he instructed them in their walk with God and with one another:

> Put on then, as God's chosen ones, holy and beloved, compassion, kindness, humility, meekness, and patience, (Colossians 3:12)

You are holy! Can you believe that? How often we see ourselves through the eyes of our enemy or through our own feelings, rather than through the eyes of God. He tells us, as He tells the church at Colossae, that we are holy; we are free from sin. We, too, are "other" than those around us; we, too, are pure; and we, too, are set apart for God.

HOLY IS "SET APART"

When our Lord taught His disciples to pray, He encouraged them to pray "hallowed be Thy Name." The name of God is set apart to be worshiped. It is never to be used in any other way, whether it is cursing or it is casual. The name of God is set above all other names and apart for only one purpose: the worship that is fitting for Him. That is the nature of holiness; it is being set apart for the purposes of God. We see this truth in the design of the priestly garments made for Aaron:

> They made the plate of the holy crown of pure gold, and wrote on it an inscription, like the engraving of a signet, "Holy to the LORD." (Exodus 39:30)

The garments and the ornaments for Aaron and the priests who would serve with him were set apart to the Lord. They represented the priests who were themselves set apart for the Lord. That is true for you and me as well. We have been made holy. Our nature is "other" than those around us; we are free from sin; and we are set apart for God's purposes in His Church. The Apostle Peter wrote about that glorious truth in his first letter:

> But you are a chosen race, a royal priesthood, a holy nation, a people for his own possession, that you may proclaim the excellencies of him who called you out of darkness into his marvelous light. (1 Peter 2:9)

We can understand this truth more fully as we look at Paul's exhortation for us to present the parts of our body to God to be used in ministry. He taught us that we died with Christ and are raised with Him as well. He called us to give ourselves to God as those alive from the dead (Rom. 6:1-18). Then, in summary, he says:

> I am speaking in human terms, because of your natural limitations. For just as you once presented your members as slaves to impurity and to lawlessness leading to more lawlessness, so now present your members as slaves to righteousness leading to sanctification. (Romans 6:19)

The righteousness of God in our lives leads to holy living! He declared us free from guilt and sin, He changed our nature so that we are "other" than those in this world, and He has set us apart for the purposes of His Kingdom. We walk in His holiness when we set our bodies and ourselves apart for God's purposes in His Church as well.

TIMES AND DATES

When the Apostle Paul wrote to the church at Thessalonica, he talked to them about "times and dates." It seems that even in the Early Church there were those who focused on speculations of the Lord's return. Paul did not feel the need to respond to those who wanted more information about those details:

> Now concerning the times and the seasons, brothers, you have no need to have anything written to you. For you yourselves are fully aware that the day of the Lord will come like a thief in the night. (1 Thessalonians 5:1-2)

Rather than responding to their request for "times and dates," Paul reminded them that The Day of the Lord will come like a "thief in the night." Unexpectedly, when so many are unprepared, when we are caught up with day-to-day interests and responsibilities, the Lord will come. While people rest confidently in their circumstances and secure in this world, destruction will come upon this earth:

> While people are saying, "There is peace and security," then sudden destruction will come upon them as labor pains come upon a pregnant woman, and they will not escape. (1 Thessalonians 5:3)

The Word of God has called us throughout history to seek peace and safety in Him alone. For those who refuse to do that, the destruction that The Day of the Lord will bring to this earth will come as suddenly as labor pains on a pregnant woman. Just as a pregnancy builds relentlessly until labor pains suddenly overcome the mother-to-be, time is building until its fullness is culminated in the Second Coming of Christ. There will be no escape for those who refused to place their faith in Him and lived in rebellion toward God and His Kingdom:

> But you are not in darkness, brothers, for that day to surprise you like a thief. For you are all children of light, children of the day. We are not of the night or of the darkness. (1 Thessalonians 5:4-5)

In contrast to those who live in darkness and face destruction, the children of the light will not be surprised by The Day of the Lord. It will not come upon us like a thief. We are sons and daughters of the day and do not belong to the night. Those who love the night are able to hide their evil deeds in the darkness of the night. In the light, everything is revealed. Those who love the light are not afraid for their lives nor that their deeds might be known:

> So then let us not sleep, as others do, but let us keep awake and be sober. (1 Thessalonians 5:6)

As Paul urges us to "not be like others," he is reminding us of the call to holiness. We are separated from the world and set aside for God and His purposes. Those in rebellion are "asleep" in terms of their preparation for The Day of the Lord; we are to be alert and "self-controlled." Living in obedience to our Lord, we focus our lives, our bodies and our desires into the fulfillment of His Kingdom:

> For those who sleep, sleep at night, and those who get drunk, are drunk at night. But since we belong to the day, let us be sober, having put on the breastplate of faith and love, and for a helmet the hope of salvation. (1 Thessalonians 5:7-8)

Paul here addresses two primary aspects of our "hiding" in this world. Sleep and drunkenness are common ways of escape for those who love the night. Living lives of denial, oblivious to reality, they will be surprised by the Day that will come like a thief. But we belong to the day, not living in denial but preparing in holiness; we are alert and controlled. Walking in the faith and love which guard our hearts and the hope of God which covers our heads, we are ready, serving the Lord with all of our hearts:

> For God has not destined us for wrath, but to obtain salvation through our Lord Jesus Christ, who died for us so that whether we are awake or asleep we might live with him. (1 Thessalonians 5:9-10)

We have not been appointed by God to suffer the wrath of The Day of the Lord. Our Father called us to receive the salvation God prepared for us in His Son. His death broke down every barrier between God and us, so that, whatever the circumstances of our lives, we may live in relationship with our Lord. We enjoy the fullness of His power and grace which flow out of His great love for us:

> Therefore encourage one another and build one another up, just as you are doing. (1 Thessalonians 5:11)

In light of the Day approaching and the provisions of our Father's love for us, our focus as we wait for our Lord to return must be to encourage one another. We should give ourselves to building up each other. It is only through encouragement and the building up of one another that we can help each other prepare for The Day of the Lord.

THE HOUR HAS COME

Paul wrote to the church at Rome in the very same way that he taught the church at Thessalonica. If we understand the times in which we live, our response will be to live in preparation to meet our Bridegroom:

> Besides this you know the time, that the hour has come for you to wake from sleep. For salvation is nearer to us now than when we first believed. (Romans 13:11)

These are not the days to sleep. Our salvation, the fulfillment of God's provisions for us in His Son, is closer now than ever before. Now is the time to wake from our slumber and live in the light, working with all our hearts in the building of His Kingdom:

> The night is far gone; the day is at hand. So then let us cast off the works of darkness and put on the armor of light. (Romans 13:12)

The darkness of this world is about to end in the return of our Lord and the dawn of a new day where His light will reign is about to appear. In light of the hope that we find in Him, the only sensible response is to lay aside the acts of darkness that characterized our former lives. Clothing ourselves in the protection of the light, we live in the holiness that expresses our Father's heart and builds His Kingdom:

> Let us walk properly as in the daytime, not in orgies and drunkenness, not in sexual immorality and sensuality, not in quarreling and jealousy. (Romans 13:13)

When we are children of the light, our behavior reflects the light. The deeds that are done in the darkness by children of the night no longer fit the desires of our hearts or the holiness of our God. Surprisingly, Paul places dissension and jealousy right there in the midst of blatant sexual sins. Anything less than the holiness of God in the lives of His children reflects the darkness of this world:

> But put on the Lord Jesus Christ, and make no provision for the flesh, to gratify its desires. (Romans 13:14)

Holiness calls us to live at the highest level of obedience concerning our nature and our desires. When we clothe ourselves with Christ and walk in obedience to Him, our passions are satisfied not in the pursuits of the flesh but in pleasing the Lord who gave Himself for us.

AHAZ, AN EVIL KING

As I have read through the Old Testament, the records of the kings of Judah have intrigued me. There were three kinds of kings that reigned over God's people. Some were evil, some were good, and one was righteous. The first type of king is seen in King Ahaz:

> Ahaz was twenty years old when he began to reign, and he reigned sixteen years in Jerusalem. And he did not do what was right in the eyes of the LORD, as his father David had done, but he walked in the ways of the kings of Israel. He even made metal images for the Baals, (2 Chronicles 28:1-2)

David is the standard by which all the other kings were measured. David, even in his failure and sin, was a "man after God's own heart" (1 Sam 13:14). He walked in obedience before the Lord and served Him with a whole heart. He loved God passionately and gave us some of the most beautiful songs of worship in the Scriptures:

> because David did what was right in the eyes of the LORD and did not turn aside from anything that he commanded him all the days of his life, except in the matter of Uriah the Hittite. (1 Kings 15:5)

Ahaz was not like David; he followed the path of the evil kings of Israel. Not one of the kings of Israel—the northern kingdom of God's people—followed the Lord. The wicked king Ahaz walked in their ways. He gave himself to the gods of the surrounding nations, making idols and worshiping Baal:

> ...he made offerings in the Valley of the Son of Hinnom and burned his sons as an offering, according to the abominations of

the nations whom the LORD drove out before the people of Israel. (2 Chronicles 28:3)

Ahaz was so wicked that he even practiced child sacrifice. He gave his own sons to the fires of sacrifice, living just as the nations that occupied the land of Israel before God gave it to His people:

> And he sacrificed and made offerings on the high places and on the hills and under every green tree. (2 Chronicles 28:4)

God commanded His people to bring offerings and sacrifices to His temple in Jerusalem. That is where He dwelt and placed His Name. But the people of Israel and Judah began to offer sacrifices in the "high places," the surrounding hills. Here they would sometimes offer sacrifices to God in disobedience to His Word, and often they would worship idols and the gods of their enemies. Ahaz followed that pattern of disobedience; he was an evil king.

HEZEKIAH, A RIGHTEOUS KING

Hezekiah was Ahaz's son, and he was completely different from his father. Hezekiah was the most righteous king in all of Judah's history:

> Hezekiah began to reign when he was twenty-five years old, and he reigned twenty-nine years in Jerusalem. His mother's name was Abijah the daughter of Zechariah. And he did what was right in the eyes of the LORD, according to all that David his father had done. (2 Chronicles 29:1-2)

Hezekiah did what was right in the eyes of the Lord. He walked in obedience before the Lord and tore down the idols and the high places that his own father had built. The writer of the Kings says this about Hezekiah:

And he did what was right in the eyes of the LORD, according to all that David his father had done. He removed the high places and broke the pillars and cut down the Asherah. And he broke in pieces the bronze serpent that Moses had made, for until those days the people of Israel had made offerings to it (it was called Nehushtan). (2 Kings 18:3-4)

Asherah was a female deity that Judah had come to worship. Hezekiah tore them down. "Nehushtan" was the name that His people had given the bronze serpent in the wilderness that God provided when His people were being bitten by poisonous snakes. God had designed it to point to His healing mercies and His grace (Num. 21:4-9), but Israel turned it into one more god to worship. That is the nature of idol worship. We take resources that our Father provides in His grace and try to turn them into sources of life themselves, even though they are empty and can bring no life. God has told us from the beginning that He is the only source of life:

He trusted in the LORD the God of Israel, so that there was none like him among all the kings of Judah after him, nor among those who were before him. (2 Kings 18:5)

No other king in Judah's history measured up to the standard of King Hezekiah. He was a righteous king who trusted in the Lord with all his heart and walked in obedience before him.

JEHOSHAPHAT, A GOOD KING

There was another kind of king in Judah's history: Jehoshaphat. He is one of my favorite characters in the Bible. We read in 2 Chronicles chapter twenty about a battle that took place between Judah and a coalition of three of its enemies. Judah was terribly outnumbered, and Jehoshaphat humbled himself before the Lord and led his people in prayer as they sought the Lord's deliverance. He followed the counsel of the prophets who reminded them that the battle was the Lord's and appointed a worship team to lead them into the battle where God gave them one of the most glorious victories in all of their history. I would encourage you to read 2 Chronicles 20. It will encourage you and fill your heart with hope. This is the summary statement of Jehoshaphat's life and reign:

> He walked in the way of Asa his father and did not turn aside from it, doing what was right in the sight of the LORD. The high places, however, were not taken away; the people had not yet set their hearts upon the God of their fathers. (2 Chronicles 20:32-33)

Jehoshaphat was a good king. He prayed, he trusted the Lord, and he worshiped. But he had a divided heart before the Lord. He did not tear down the high places of idol worship or lead his people to seek the Lord with whole hearts.

We have, then, these three types of kings in Judah's history, typified by the three men we just looked at. Ahaz was an evil king; Hezekiah was a righteous king; and Jehoshaphat was a good king. Which of these three do you most identify with? Some people live in outright rebellion before the Lord and seek evil at every opportunity. They give themselves wholeheartedly to idols. Others are wholehearted in their service and obedience before the Lord. Then there are those who are good, who pray, humble themselves before the Lord and worship. But they do not tear down the high places in their hearts or remove the idols that they have worshiped.

TEARING DOWN HIGH PLACES

What are the high places that we allow to remain where we worship other gods? What are the idols that we serve? An idol is anything less than God which has captivated our worship. Or it might be something that God gives us as a resource of His love and grace that we turn instead into a source of life. For some of us, that might be our sexual desires; for others it might be a love for material things. It might be our hope in our retirement plan or our love for our ministry or our career. These might be outright sins like our lusts and our pride, anger and bitterness, gossiping and slander. Or we might have set up as an idol the image of an ideal marriage or family. These are high places where we are worshiping idols rather than seeking the Lord and worshiping Him alone.

I know which of these three kings I identify with. I am like Jehoshaphat. I have prayed, I have humbled myself, and I have worshiped. There are high places, however, that I have allowed to remain in my heart. My parents were the angriest people I have ever known. Before they were converted, they could spend hours on end calling each other the vilest names they could think of. This is a "sin of my fathers" that I have struggled with, but it is my sin as well. I embraced it and gave myself to it. When God in His mercy saved me, He changed me, and I grew in His grace over the years as I have walked with Him. But even when I feel that I have dealt with the sins of my past, sometimes that angry spirit is there. It is a "high place" that I have allowed to remain in my heart.

Just this past summer, my wife Karen and I were at their family's summer home in Michigan for a few days. One morning, there was something that I desired and hoped Karen would do for me. In another situation it could have been many things, but this time it was only a cup of coffee. I had hinted but did not express myself clearly. Karen did not pick up on it, and I began to feel sorry for myself rather than come right out and ask her. It is difficult for me to confess that one of the high places that I have allowed to remain in my heart and one of the idols that I have come to worship is self pity. It is childish, and it is ugly. After I pouted for a while, I made an angry comment to Karen. Now Karen is a beautiful, godly woman with a quiet spirit, but that morning she met my angry, selfish comment with some harsh words of her own, words I needed to hear. Later on, she said, "Well, at least the neighbors know us better now."

One of the things that made David a "man after God's own heart" was his spirit of repentance. I needed to repent of my sin, just as David did (Ps. 51). That is part of walking in obedience. In his excellent book *Holiness by Grace*, Bryan Chapell talks of obedience and repentance:

> Though the Bible does not teach that obedience is a condition of God's pardon, it cautions against thinking that God will forgive where there is no real change of heart. God is not waiting for us to fix our lives before He forgives us, for then none would be forgiven; but He does not promise forgiveness where repentance is not sincere. While we should not delay until we have corrected our sin, we also should not think that God will accept repentance from a heart still in rebellion against Him. If repentance is only a tool to manipulate God into averting the consequences of our wrongdoing, without any real intention of changing our ways, then we should remember that God will not hear those who cherish sin in their heart.[10]

I have walked with the Lord for many years now, and I desire to serve Him with all my heart. In order to do that, I know that I need a higher level of obedience before Him. I need to tear down the high places and break down the idols that I have come to worship.

---

[10]Bryan Chappell, *Holiness by Grace: Delighting in the Joy that Is Our Strength*, (Wheaton: Crossway Books, 2001), p. 87

The Day of the Lord!

Perhaps you sense that reality in your own heart as well as you study these Scriptures with me. Would you spend time in prayer asking God what high places remain in your life? What idols are you serving that draw your heart away from the Lord? Since our Lord will soon appear and everything will be destroyed, let us be like King Hezekiah and King David. May we live holy and godly lives as we are preparing to meet our Bridegroom!

SPEED THE DAY'S COMING

> what sort of people ought you to be in lives of holiness and godliness, waiting for and hastening the coming of the day of God, (2 Peter 3:11b-12a)

Peter links the living of holy lives with looking forward to The Day of The Lord. He also calls us to "speed its coming." How can we speed the Lord's return? Isn't the date of the Second Coming set in the sovereignty of God's eternal purposes? Can we really move up the date of our Lord's return by living godly lives and serving in missions and evangelism?

Jesus clearly tells us that the Father knows the day of His return (Matt. 24:36; Mark 13:32). Peter teaches us that we participate in the preparation of God's purposes to be fulfilled in that Day as we walk before Him in obedience and share His heart for missions and evangelism. This is an awesome and amazing truth! Jesus touched on this when He told His disciples about the relationship between evangelism, missions and The Day of the Lord.

> And this gospel of the kingdom will be proclaimed throughout the whole world as a testimony to all nations, and then the end will come. (Matthew 24:14)

I am revealing my bias here. As I said in the introduction of this book, all of the details of prophetic teaching are critically important. As the people of God, we need to be reminded, even as Peter is reminding us in this Scripture, of the things the prophets foretold. But at the same time, please permit me to say that only in the affluent and distracted developed nations do we have the time, energy and funds to spend on the speculations of dates, times, and the placement of nations. If we would, however, focus the investment of our hearts, our strength, and our funds in prayer for the nations, holy living, missions, and evangelism, we would be a church far better prepared to meet her Bridegroom.

GROUP STUDY GUIDE
AND PERSONAL APPLICATION

1. When Peter talks about the heavens disappearing and the elements being destroyed, how are your hopes for the future affected? How does this thought touch your fears?

2. How does the idea of everything being "laid bare" affect our nature to hide? Could the thought of everything in our lives being exposed create even more fear than the reality of the elements melting?

3. Which of the three aspects of God's holiness creates in you the greatest sense of worship? When you look at them, where do you need to grow the most?

4. Paul called us to be "self-controlled." How have you seen God develop that character quality in your life?

5. As you look back over your life, how have you seen God transform you from a person "sleeping in the darkness" to a child of the light?

6. The Scriptures teach us that the way to deal with the desires of our sinful nature is to "clothe ourselves with the Lord Jesus Christ." What does that mean? How do you do that?

7. Of the three kings that we studied, which one do you most identify with? Why?

8. What are some of the "high places" that you have allowed to remain in your life? What are some of the idols that still have not been torn down? What instructions do the Scriptures give in order to deal with the high places and the idols?

REFLECTIONS, COMMITMENTS AND PRAYER

Perhaps the teaching of the Scriptures about the end of the earth and the heavens does bring fear to our hearts, instead of causing us to look forward to the new heavens and earth that we will inherit. Ask God to bring comfort to your heart and increase your confidence in Him. Pray that He will give you an even greater hunger for holiness and teach you to live as a child of the light. Confess to the Lord the "high places" that remain in your life. Commit yourself before Him to tear down the idols that have remained, perhaps for generations, in your family and in your heart. Ask God to enable you to live a righteous life before Him, even as Hezekiah did, for the glory of His Kingdom.

But according to his promise we are waiting for new heavens and a new earth in which righteousness dwells.

2 Peter 3:13

6

Heaven: God's Home of Righteousness

Earlier in our study, we talked about "going home." In John 14:1-3, the Lord Jesus talked to His disciples about going to prepare a place for them in the Father's house and then coming back for them, taking them to live with Him in that house forever. That house will be in a new heaven and a new earth, and it will be the home of righteousness.

How evil this world must be that God has to destroy it in order to prepare a place where "righteousness dwells!" When we try to visualize the cataclysm that Peter describes in the destruction of the heavens and the earth, we cannot even begin to grasp the fullness of the devastation. The heavens will disappear with a roar, the elements will melt in the heat, and the earth will be destroyed. God will do all of this to judge the wickedness in this world and to bring the hope to His children of an entirely new world where His righteousness will reign.

Dick Lucas and Christopher Green, in their book *The Message of 2 Peter and Jude; The Promise of His Coming*, give us some understanding of the need for this complete devastation of the present earth and heaven:

> Peter sees, then, that all of the elements of the universe, which in our terms range from subatomic particles through the vast interstellar systems, will be destroyed by fire. This blistering destruction is so unimaginably vast that we begin to see how futile it is to think we can bring about Christ's Kingdom by mere revolution or social change, however desirable change may be. Nor could anything so relatively small as a global nuclear holocaust or climate change account for the universal melt down that Peter envisages. Yet nothing less than that will accomplish God's purpose for a new creation.[11]

The Entire Creation Is Groaning

For us to experience and inherit something so new and so glorious as a home of righteousness, God must do away with the present realities of this age. As Lucas and Green said, social change or revolution will not accomplish God's purposes in His new creation. He desires a place where the righteousness and justice that fill His heart will also fill His world.

Think with me for a moment of our experience in the "new creation." We have already tasted it and lived in it even while in this world. What actually happened to us when we were "born again?" The person that we were died, and God created an entirely new person to live in its place:

---

[11]Dick Lucas and Christopher Green, *The Message of 2 Peter and Jude; The Promise of His Coming*, (Downers Grove, IL: InterVarsity Press, 1995), pp. 142-143.

> Therefore, if anyone is in Christ, he is a new creation. The old has passed away; behold, the new has come. (2 Corinthians 5:17)

In his letter to the Romans, the Apostle Paul taught us more fully about our walk in the new creation while we are still present in this world. He teaches us in the sixth chapter of his letter that we were "united with Christ in His death and resurrection" (Rom. 6:5-7). Paul then exhorts us to walk in the new creation by presenting our bodies and ourselves to the Lord:

> Let not sin therefore reign in your mortal bodies, to make you obey their passions. Do not present your members to sin as instruments for unrighteousness, but present yourselves to God as those who have been brought from death to life, and your members to God as instruments for righteousness. (Romans 6:12-13)

Why is it so critical for us to present the parts of our bodies to the Lord? If we would be His servants in this world, we need to give our bodies over to Him. Rather than following our old pattern of presenting the parts of our bodies as instruments of sin, we now present them to God to be used as weapons of ministry. We need to do this because our bodies did not share in the recreation experience that was ours in the new creation. When we were converted and placed our faith in Christ, our persons died and were recreated, but our bodies did not change. They did not share in the recreation process. Our mortal bodies are still made of the stuff of this world and are still in the process of dying. The law of sin and death is still reigning in our bodies while a new law, "the law of the spirit of life," is now reigning in our inner persons:

> There is therefore now no condemnation for those who are in Christ Jesus. For the law of the Spirit of life has set you free in Christ Jesus from the law of sin and death. (Romans 8:1-2)

Paul brings us, then, to the hope of the new creation, not only for us, but also for this entire world. Remember when we looked at the "eternal weight of glory" that Paul talked about in 2 Corinthians 4? How he encouraged us with the knowledge that our momentary troubles are producing for us an eternal glory that far outweighs what we are experiencing now! He comes back to that theme in his letter to the church at Rome:

> For I consider that the sufferings of this present time are not worth comparing with the glory that is to be revealed to us. For the creation waits with eager longing for the revealing of the sons of God. (Romans 8:18-19)

We, as the children of God, are suffering in the midst of this pain-filled world where injustice reigns. But there will be a glory revealed in us, Paul says, far beyond our present afflictions which often seem more than we can bear. Then he sets before us that incredible truth: the creation is waiting in "eager expectation" for us as God's sons and daughters to be revealed:

> For the creation was subjected to futility, not willingly, but because of him who subjected it, in hope that the creation itself will be set free from its bondage to decay and obtain the freedom of the glory of the children of God. (Romans 8:20-21)

When Adam fell, all of creation fell. His sin did not affect only Adam and Eve and their children. Their sin caused the reign of sin and death to come upon all of God's creation. The hope of creation is to someday share in what we have already experienced! Just as we have been set free from the law of sin and death and tasted of the new creation, this world is waiting to experience that transforming new life as well. The liberation from bondage and decay that is ours in Christ will someday flow through the heavens and the earth:

For we know that the whole creation has been groaning together in the pains of childbirth until now. (Romans 8:22)

The pain of a fallen world overwhelmed all of the present creation. What a woman experiences in the pain of childbirth is shared by the entire physical world. This creation is "groaning" in its pain and in its desire for new life:

And not only the creation, but we ourselves, who have the firstfruits of the Spirit, groan inwardly as we wait eagerly for adoption as sons, the redemption of our bodies. (Romans 8:23)

WHY THE WAIT?

We are groaning, too, Paul says. We have already experienced the "first fruits of the Spirit." We have tasted of God's resurrection life and the liberation which come in the new creation. In our inner person, we have been set free from bondage and decay, and we are enjoying the glorious freedom that is ours in Christ. In the sovereignty of God's timing, however, He chose for our bodies not to share in that recreation process. Because He designed our bodies as the perfect tools to proclaim His glory and pour out His life in this world, God ordained for us to remain in these physical bodies that are still in need of redemption.

I have grown to know and love Joni Eareckson Tada through her ministry, "Joni and Friends." Joni is a quadriplegic. When Joni was seventeen years old, she injured her spinal column in a diving accident, and has been in a wheelchair ever since. Joni is a glorious example of Paul's teaching to the church at Corinth. He says:

So we do not lose heart. Though our outer nature is wasting away, our inner nature is being renewed day by day. (2 Corinthians 4:16)

143

Joni's beauty and radiance are the overflow of God's renewing work within her by His Holy Spirit. Even though she battles with physical disabilities, God is using her to touch the lives of countless thousands with His healing love and grace. In her wonderfully encouraging book titled *Heaven*, Joni talks about looking forward to her new body in the resurrection:

> One day the dream will come true.
> One day, if I should die before Jesus returns, my soul will be reunited with my body. Pause and dream with me....
> One day no more bulging middles or balding tops. No varicose veins or crow's-feet. No more cellulite or support hose. Forget the thunder thighs and highway hips. Just a quick leapfrog over the tombstone and it's the body you've always dreamed of. Fit and trim, smooth and sleek.
> It makes me want to break up into giggles right now! Little wonder "we eagerly await a Savior from [heaven], the Lord Jesus Christ, who, by the power that enables him to bring everything under his control, will transform our lowly bodies so that they will be like his glorious body" (Philippians 3:20-21).
> *Our lowly bodies...will be like His glorious body.* Astounding. Like Jesus in His resurrected body, we will have hands and arms, feet and legs. We won't be spirit beings, floating around like angels who have no bodies.[12]

Why did God leave us in a body like Joni describes, one which bears all of the fallenness of this world and the ravages of time? Surely, He could have given us a new body immediately when we

---

[12]Joni Eareckson Tada, *Heaven: Your Real Home*, (Grand Rapids, MI: Zondervan Publishing House, 1995), pp. 34-35.

were saved. Just as our inner person died and was recreated in the twinkling of an eye when we were born again, God could have recreated our body just like that at the same time. Why are we waiting and groaning now?

BETWEEN TWO WORLDS

The body in which we live is the point of contact between two worlds, where the physical realm and the eternal Kingdom of God touch one another. Through our lips God speaks His eternal words that bring life, encouragement, and hope to lost people. Through our hands God reaches out to touch those in pain with His healing love. Through our eyes we see people the way He sees them, with all of the value that flows from being made in His image and all of their worth found in the Father's eyes. Through our feet God brings the gospel to the nations.

Our bodies are the perfectly designed vessels through which God is pouring out His life in this world. But our bodies have not been redeemed. They have not died and been raised to new life. That will be our experience in the resurrection. Now, with all of creation, we are waiting for the fulfillment of our adoption in Christ Jesus, the redemption of our bodies. In the meantime, like the rest of creation, we are groaning with all of the bondage and decay of this physical world:

> For in this hope we were saved. Now hope that is seen is not hope. For who hopes for what he sees? But if we hope for what we do not see, we wait for it with patience. (Romans 8:24-25)

When we first came to trust in Christ, this was our very hope, Paul says. The hope of freedom, redemption and resurrection was at the center of our faith. But, as Paul says, who hopes for what they already possess? We face the future with confident hope, built strongly on the foundation of God who keeps His

Word. Our secure hope will be fulfilled in the resurrection. But now we wait patiently for its fulfillment in The Day of the Lord.

LORD, PLEASE COME DOWN!

Part of that waiting process is bearing not only the pain and affliction that touch us physically, but the great injustice of this world. Throughout history, the people of God have hungered for His righteousness to reign. This was the cry of the prophet Isaiah:

> Oh that you would rend the heavens and come down, that the mountains might quake at your presence—as when fire kindles brushwood and the fire causes water to boil—to make your name known to your adversaries, and that the nations might tremble at your presence! (Isaiah 64:1-2)

This has been the cry of many of us as well. If God would just enter time and put an end to the hatred and destruction of this world, bring about the reign of His justice and put away the evil doers, this world would be a much better place. That was the hope of the disciples when they wanted Jesus to establish His Kingdom in this world. They failed to understand that His Kingdom was not of this world but of hearts controlled by His Spirit. There will be a much better world. God is going to create a whole new world, where His righteousness will reign. Wouldn't you like to live in a world where everything was done right?

The prophet Isaiah saw a vision of this New World. In a completely new order of power and relationships, one in which justice and righteousness will produce an entirely different nature of ruling, the glory of God will be revealed. It will be in every way the "flip-side" of this present world:

> The word that Isaiah the son of Amoz saw concerning Judah and Jerusalem. It shall come to pass in the latter days that the

mountain of the house of the LORD shall be established as the highest of the mountains, and shall be lifted up above the hills; and all the nations shall flow to it, (Isaiah 2:1-2)

Someday, the temple of the Lord will be established in this world. His laws will not only govern the nations, they will be written on the hearts of all mankind. All the nations will flock to the house of the Lord to learn how to live and to worship:

and many peoples shall come, and say: "Come, let us go up to the mountain of the LORD, to the house of the God of Jacob, that he may teach us his ways and that we may walk in his paths." For out of Zion shall go the law, and the word of the LORD from Jerusalem. (Isaiah 2:3)

The peoples of the world will hunger to be taught by God. There will be no resistance, no lack of interest and no competition for their hearts. After a history filled with violence, the nations will hunger to know God's ways. Men and women everywhere will want to walk in His paths. The law of God will flow out from His dwelling place and His Word from the city where He placed His Name:

He shall judge between the nations, and shall decide disputes for many peoples; and they shall beat their swords into plowshares, and their spears into pruning hooks; nation shall not lift up sword against nation, neither shall they learn war anymore. (Isaiah 2:4)

God Himself will be the judge of all the earth, and His words will arbitrate between men and women. We will run to transform our weapons of war into tools for planting and harvesting. The swords that have set nation against nation will be laid down, and no longer will we train for war. God's peace will rule in the new heaven and the new earth. We will hunger to learn peace and to walk in the ways of the Lord:

The Day of the Lord!

> O house of Jacob, come, let us walk in the light of the LORD. (Isaiah 2:5)

LET JUSTICE ROLL ON

We must be careful not to "settle in" with the wickedness around us while we are still living in this world. Even while we are waiting for God to bring in the new heavens and the new earth, we are called to pursue righteousness and justice. Sometimes, like the children of Israel, we fall into patterns of religious activity that reflect the ways of this world rather than the heart of God. Through His prophet Amos, God confronted the nation's lack of righteousness in light of The Day of the Lord:

> Woe to you who desire the day of the LORD! Why would you have the day of the LORD? It is darkness, and not light, (Amos 5:18)

Israel longed for The Day of the Lord. They saw it as their release from slavery and the redemption of their nation. Amos, however, told them that the Day would bring darkness rather than light. For those living in darkness and rebellion against God, there is good reason to fear The Day of the Lord:

> as if a man fled from a lion, and a bear met him, or went into the house and leaned his hand against the wall, and a serpent bit him. Is not the day of the LORD darkness, and not light, and gloom with no brightness in it? (Amos 5:19-20)

Amos 3 paints a graphic description of people running away from those things that we fear will devour us, hoping for deliverance, but facing something even more frightening. Can you imagine escaping from a lion, feeling safe for only a moment before confronting a bear? Or feeling safe in your own home only to be bitten by a poisonous serpent? The depth of the darkness that Amos pictures is one where hearts are consumed with fear and emptied of hope. Such will be The Day of the Lord for those who refuse to place their hope in God!

God links the hopelessness which His people face in The Day of the Lord to their religious expressions. Even though they observed religious rituals, they were hopeless before the righteous God:

> I hate, I despise your feasts, and I take no delight in your solemn assemblies. (Amos 5:21)

The very things that God sought from His people, He now rejected as worthless. He called them to these very sacrifices and festivals. But He required them to come before Him in their religious observances with a sincere heart. They, however, went only through the motions of their religion without examining their hearts. What God once loved to receive from His people, their offerings and their sacrifices, He came to hate:

> Even though you offer me your burnt offerings and grain offerings, I will not accept them; and the peace offerings of your fattened animals, I will not look upon them. Take away from me the noise of your songs; to the melody of your harps I will not listen. (Amos 5:22-23)

God despised the observances of their worship. He hated their feasts. He could not stand their assemblies and would not accept their offerings. What harsh language! We cannot imagine God using more descriptive words to let His people know how little regard He had for their religious activities. Then He told them what He really desired:

> But let justice roll down like waters, and righteousness like an ever-flowing stream. (Amos 5:24)

Justice and righteousness are the evidence of God's Kingdom and what He desires from His people. The sacrifices and festivals that God instituted for Israel were to be outward expressions of inwardly transformed hearts. Without the humility and repentance of a sincere heart before the holy God, the sacrifices and offerings of His people became only more "religious stuff" they flaunted in His presence, until He had enough and cast them out of His presence.

This Scripture causes me to examine my own heart in light of my religious activities and pursuit of justice. Do we, like Israel, fall into the motions of religious stuff without expressing the heart of God in our commitments to righteousness in this world? If we are not involved in ministries of compassion for the poor, seeking what is right for the hurting people of this world, and elevating those who have been pushed down, our religion is in vain. If we are not reaching out to the imprisoned and forgotten, and remembering the weak, we are not reflecting the heart of God and advancing His Kingdom. If justice is not "rolling down" from our lives and our churches, I think God feels about us and our religion just like He did about His people described in the book of Amos.

His Kingdom Is Now

How do we prepare for heaven, a place where "righteousness dwells?" We do that by pursuing the righteousness of God in our own lives through faith in His Son, who shed His blood for our sins on the cross of Calvary. We prepare for our eternal home, too, by pursuing justice in this world as we advance the Kingdom of God right now.

Jesus introduced His Kingdom to His disciples early in His ministry to them. In the book of Matthew, in what has come to be known as the "Sermon on the Mount," we see that the multitudes began to gather around Jesus but He focused His message on the few that He had called to be His servants in a new Kingdom:

> Seeing the crowds, he went up on the mountain, and when he sat down, his disciples came to him. And he opened his mouth and taught them, saying: (Matthew 5:1-2)

The Lord Jesus had just healed many people with a variety of diseases (Matt. 4:23-25) and cast out demons. He spoke with such authority that the multitudes crowded around Him. They hung on every word that came from His lips. Then came the pronouncement that must have stunned His audience. Time is intersecting with eternity as we listen in. Christ's words surely brought the angels to rapt attention and caused them to worship:

> Blessed are the poor in spirit, for theirs is the kingdom of heaven. (Matthew 5:3)

Jesus is calling His disciples to an attitude of humility, one in which they see themselves through the eyes of God. He is telling them that the only way they can come to God is like a beggar, with their hands held open wide. They are spiritually bankrupt apart from Him and desperately in need of His mercy and His grace. They bring nothing to Him that will commend them in His presence. If they come before the Father with a spirit like that, the Kingdom of heaven is theirs right now:

> Blessed are those who mourn, for they shall be comforted. Blessed are the meek, for they shall inherit the earth. (Matthew 5:4-5)

Other attitudes are now confronted. Jesus talks about brokenness over sin and grieving before the Lord because of their rebellion, pride and independence. He describes attitudes of gentleness that flow from the heart of a servant:

> Blessed are those who hunger and thirst for righteousness, for they shall be satisfied. Blessed are the merciful, for they shall receive mercy. (Matthew 5:6-7)

Jesus continued to teach about heart attitudes. Perhaps His audience had fallen into the same religious rituals without life that we read about in Amos' prophecies. He talks about being hungry for righteousness in order to be filled up. He calls His hearers to give away the heart of God in mercy and forgiveness if they desire mercy from Him:

> Blessed are the pure in heart, for they shall see God. Blessed are the peacemakers, for they shall be called sons of God. (Matthew 5:8-9)

Now our Lord turns to desires for holiness. He tells the disciples that if they hope to see God, their hearts need to be pure before Him. Jesus calls them to make peace. How will the world know that they are God's children? If they seek to make peace at any cost, they will be like their Father in heaven. And then we hear that amazing word again:

> Blessed are those who are persecuted for righteousness' sake, for theirs is the kingdom of heaven. (Matthew 5:10)

For the second time Jesus said those remarkable words: theirs *is* the Kingdom of heaven! Right now, right here, theirs *is* the Kingdom of heaven. Jesus is talking about a present reality, not something that His disciples will experience when they die. The very moment faith is transferred from this world to Christ and His Kingdom, His Kingdom becomes our kingdom, a place where we will find our identity and our fulfillment, our security and our hope. Paul also talked about how our lives are transferred from one kingdom to another in this way:

He has delivered us from the domain of darkness and transferred us to the kingdom of his beloved Son, in whom we have redemption, the forgiveness of sins. (Colossians 1:13-14)

The inauguration of God's Kingdom had just taken place as
Jesus spoke the Beatitudes to His disciples in Matthew 5. It is not
a political system, even though it governs political systems. It is
not a country in this world, nor a throne that sits in a palace. This
reign does not originate in a castle. One day, however, His throne
will sit in Jerusalem in the new heavens and earth. Now, it is a
rule in the hearts of people who seek God and humble themselves in His presence. The Kingdom of God is seen in the new attitudes of transformed desires and relationships.

Christ's Kingdom was inaugurated in His First Coming and
now rules in the hearts of those who serve Him. We also look for
the physical reign of Jesus in this world. The Apostle John
foretold of that reign with those who were martyred in His
name:

Then I saw thrones, and seated on them were those to whom the
authority to judge was committed. Also I saw the souls of those
who had been beheaded for the testimony of Jesus and for the
word of God, and who had not worshiped the beast or its image
and had not received its mark on their foreheads or their hands.
They came to life and reigned with Christ for a thousand years.
The rest of the dead did not come to life until the thousand years
were ended. This is the first resurrection. (Revelation 20:4-5)

How do we prepare to live in heaven, the home of righteousness? We prepare by living in God's Kingdom of righteousness
right now the way He teaches us to live. We seek His Kingdom
with all our hearts, we hunger for holiness, and we pursue it in
the call to justice and righteousness in the kingdoms of this

world. We walk with our Lord in the building of His eternal Kingdom right now in the realms of time and space by our obedience, our giving and our serving.

THE WHITE HORSE AND ITS RIDER

The Apostle John, in his revelation from God concerning The Day of the Lord, pictures for us the reign of righteousness in heaven. By God's Spirit, he saw heaven "standing open," and then he saw the Son of God exalted in His faithfulness and truth. The reason that heaven is the home of righteousness is because the Lord Christ judges with justice:

> Then I saw heaven opened, and behold, a white horse! The one sitting on it is called Faithful and True, and in righteousness he judges and makes war. (Revelation 19:11)

What a vision we see through the Apostle John! When I read this description of the exalted Christ, I think of those in this world that would say concerning Christians, Muslims and Jews, "We all worship the same God." I want to cry out, "Unless they worship the God who is revealed in Jesus Christ, they are worshiping a different god!"

> His eyes are like a flame of fire, and on his head are many diadems, and he has a name written that no one knows but himself. (Revelation 19:12)

The Lord Jesus Christ with blazing eyes and crowned in glory has an identity all His own. He is prepared to judge and to make war with justice. This vision of His power and glory tells us that soon all authorities in heaven and earth will bow before Him:

> He is clothed in a robe dipped in blood, and the name by which he is called is The Word of God. (Revelation 19:13)

John tells us clearly the identity of the rider on the white horse. He is the Word of God. The same Word that John told us in the first chapter of his gospel was in the beginning with God and was God (John 1:1,2). The eternal God is dressed in a robe dipped in blood. It is His own blood that provided the precious dye for that robe. The blood of Jesus that poured out of His own veins and down that wooden cross washed away all of the sins of all who would believe in Him:

> And the armies of heaven, arrayed in fine linen, white and pure, were following him on white horses. (Revelation 19:14)

Because His robe is dipped in blood, the armies of heaven are wearing robes of white. Their robes are of fine linen and clean. They, too, are riding white horses, following in His train:

> From his mouth comes a sharp sword with which to strike down the nations, and he will rule them with a rod of iron. He will tread the winepress of the fury of the wrath of God the Almighty. (Revelation 19:15)

The Apostle Paul tells us in his Ephesian letter that the sword of the Spirit is the Word of God (Eph. 6: 17). Here, John pictures for us the Living Word of God from whose mouth comes a sharp sword. With this sword Christ will strike down the nations, as He will judge and make war with justice. After His victory, Jesus will rule with a scepter of iron. Strength and authority belong to the Lord our God:

> On his robe and on his thigh he has a name written, King of kings and Lord of lords. (Revelation 19:16)

Jesus is revealed here in the fullness of His glory and power. His own name tells us; it is written on His robe and on His thigh: Jesus is "King of kings and Lord of lords." There is no authority above Him, and there is no other god. He alone is worthy; He alone is glorious; He alone is powerful; He alone will rule; and He alone will be worshiped. Heaven is the home of righteousness because the King of Righteousness is reigning there.

No More Death

John continues with his vision of the new heavens and the new earth. As Peter taught us, the first heaven and the first earth passed away, as the elements melted and everything was destroyed. Even the sea disappeared:

> Then I saw a new heaven and a new earth, for the first heaven and the first earth had passed away, and the sea was no more. (Revelation 21:1)

Now John, in his vision of all that is new, sees the new Jerusalem, the Holy City of God. It looks like a bride dressed in preparation to meet her husband:

> And I saw the holy city, new Jerusalem, coming down out of heaven from God, prepared as a bride adorned for her husband. (Revelation 21:2)

John not only sees this glorious vision; he hears a voice as well, a voice coming from the very throne of God:

> And I heard a loud voice from the throne saying, "Behold, the dwelling place of God is with man. He will dwell with them, and they will be his people, and God himself will be with them as their God." (Revelation 21:3)

We studied earlier in John 14 where Jesus told His disciples that He was going to prepare a place for them and that someday He would come back for them. They would live with Him in His eternal home forever (John 14:1-4). Later on in that same chapter, He told the disciples that in the meantime He and His Father would come and live with them where they live (John 14:23). We see in this Scripture the fulfillment of that wonderful promise:

> He will wipe away every tear from their eyes, and death shall be no more, neither shall there be mourning nor crying nor pain anymore, for the former things have passed away. (Revelation 21:4)

What will we experience in heaven, the home of righteousness? God Himself will wipe away our tears. A lifetime of hurting, disappointment and pain will be healed in a moment by the touch of our loving Father's hand. Death will be no more because our great enemy has been defeated at the cross and in the resurrection of our Lord. We will mourn and weep no more because a "new order" has been introduced in the reign of our glorious Lord:

> And he who was seated on the throne said, "Behold, I am making all things new." Also he said, "Write this down, for these words are trustworthy and true." (Revelation 21:5)

There will not only be a new heaven and a new earth, our God will make everything new. With the authority that comes from the throne itself, a new order for all things is declared. It must have been almost too much for John to grasp, for the Lord says, "Write it down. It is true; you can trust these words:"

> And he said to me, "It is done! I am the Alpha and the Omega, the beginning and the end. To the thirsty I will give from the spring of the water of life without payment. The one who conquers will have this heritage, and I will be his God and he will be my son." (Revelation 21:6-7)

When Jesus died on the cross, He said, "It is finished." The work of redemption was completed. All that needed to be accomplished to appease the Father's wrath and to bring men and women to salvation was fulfilled. Now once again we hear those words, "It is done." All that God had purposed for time has been fulfilled, and everything inside of time has been filled up and completed in Christ.

When God says, "I am the Alpha and the Omega, the Beginning and the End," I can hear Him saying, "I have everything surrounded. All of time and eternity and everything in them are now complete." And then, as God has done throughout all of time, once again He calls us to come freely and to be filled up and satisfied in Him. The ones who endure to the end and are victorious in Christ will inherit the new heavens and the new earth and live forever as a child of God:

> But as for the cowardly, the faithless, the detestable, as for murderers, the sexually immoral, sorcerers, idolaters, and all liars, their portion will be in the lake that burns with fire and sulfur, which is the second death. (Revelation 21:8)

Those who refuse to repent and believe and who have lived vile and wicked lives will suffer the "second death." God's lake of fire is their eternal destination. They go there of their own free will. Without the evil that has filled the realms of time, we will be free to worship and celebrate the glories of God for all of eternity. His presence will fill heaven, the home of righteousness.

No More Night

Toward the end of John's revelation, we see another picture that is glorious in its beauty and power. Just as God wiped away our tears, we now see the healing of the nations:

> Then the angel showed me the river of the water of life, bright as crystal, flowing from the throne of God and of the Lamb through the middle of the street of the city; also, on either side of the river, the tree of life with its twelve kinds of fruit, yielding its fruit each month. The leaves of the tree were for the healing of the nations. (Revelation 22:1-2)

The river of the water of life is flowing from the very throne of God. Since it is flowing from the life source, it is bringing life wherever it flows. On either side of this life-giving river are the trees that bear fruit each month. In their leaves is the balm that brings healing to the nations:

> No longer will there be anything accursed, but the throne of God and of the Lamb will be in it, and his servants will worship him. They will see his face, and his name will be on their foreheads. (Revelation 22:3-4)

The curse that fell upon all mankind because of Adam's sin (Gen. 3:14-24) has been lifted because God's redemption is fulfilled. God's throne will be established in the new Jerusalem, and we will be free to serve Him. We will see His face, and we will bear His name.

I remember the morning that my mother entered eternity. I watched God transform my mom from a hard, bitter, angry person into a gentle, loving woman. I saw her grow in His grace and become a wonderful grandmother to our sons Peter and Joel. Then, she suffered a heart attack. I returned quickly from a time of ministry and was able to spend a very special afternoon with her. We talked of family and good times and affirmed our love for each other. Early the next morning we received a call from the hospital. Mom had suffered another heart attack and had gone into cardiac arrest. As we watched the monitors and saw her heart rate slowing down, I bent down to her ear and said, "Mom, you are about to see His face!"

I know my mom is seeing the face of the Lord she grew to love. She is enjoying His presence and living in His home of righteousness. It will be a very brief time, and I will be there, too. How wonderful it will be to go home:

> And night will be no more. They will need no light of lamp or sun, for the Lord God will be their light, and they will reign forever and ever. (Revelation 22:5)

All that characterized the night of this world is now done away with. The evil, the darkness, the injustice and the fear are gone. This is the home of righteousness! The Lord God Himself will light His new home. We will live in His light and walk in His presence and reign with Him forever and ever.

A HOME FILLED WITH WORSHIP

When Peter and Joel were young, we lived in a rather large house. We had very special times in that house; I loved living in that home. There were so many halls to run through and so many places to hide when we played games. I loved the fireplace and the warmth it provided. What I remember best was the music, the joy and the laughter.

What will fill our new home, the home of righteousness? It will be filled with the joy and music of the greatest worship we have ever experienced! In John's revelation, he describes some of that worship for us. The scene is the throne room in heaven, and Jesus has been found worthy to open the seals and the scroll on which are written the judgments of God:

> And between the throne and the four living creatures and among the elders I saw a Lamb standing, as though it had been slain,

with seven horns and with seven eyes, which are the seven spirits of God sent out into all the earth. (Revelation 5:6)

The Lamb of God who has taken away our sins is in the center of the throne. The four living creatures and the elders surround him:

> And he went and took the scroll from the right hand of him who was seated on the throne. And when he had taken the scroll, the four living creatures and the twenty-four elders fell down before the Lamb, each holding a harp, and golden bowls full of incense, which are the prayers of the saints. (Revelation 5:7-8)

With the authority that only the eternal Son of God possesses, the Lord Jesus takes the scroll. The elders and the living creatures fall down before Him. They hold bowls of incense, which are our prayers. Isn't that one of the most glorious statements about prayer in all of the Scriptures? Are our prayers important? Do they really matter? Our prayers are eternal and precious to our Father, wafting up to the very throne room of God!:

> And they sang a new song, saying, "Worthy are you to take the scroll and to open its seals, for you were slain, and by your blood you ransomed people for God from every tribe and language and people and nation, and you have made them a kingdom and priests to our God, and they shall reign on the earth." (Revelation 5:9-10)

Worship begins now to fill the throne room. The worthiness of Jesus and His great love poured out in redemption fill His elders and the living creatures with awe and wonder. He has completed the Father's purposes, and they break forth in a new song:

> Then I looked, and I heard around the throne and the living creatures and the elders the voice of many angels, numbering myriads of myriads and thousands of thousands, saying with a loud voice, "Worthy is the Lamb who was slain, to receive power and

wealth and wisdom and might and honor and glory and blessing!" (Revelation 5:11-12)

Then John sees the multitudes, far more than anyone could number. A myriad of angels circle the throne. Their voices are like thunder. They are overwhelmed by the worthiness of the Lamb. He alone should receive all power, wealth, wisdom, strength, honor, glory and praise. No one else is worthy. Then every creature in of all the heavens and earth join in the song:

> And I heard every creature in heaven and on earth and under the earth and in the sea, and all that is in them, saying, "To him who sits on the throne and to the Lamb be blessing and honor and glory and might forever and ever!" (Revelation 5:13)

The worship builds to the most incredible crescendo. The voices we hear are those of angels and elders, fish and birds, cows and horses, elephants and whales, and those from every tribe and tongue and people and nation, all experiencing for the first time the highest purpose of their creation:

> And the four living creatures said, "Amen!" and the elders fell down and worshiped. (Revelation 5:14)

And we will be there. We will be part of that glorious throng on that day when our Lord is exalted in worship and proclaimed worthy. The song will go on for an eternity, filling heaven, the home of righteousness.

GROUP STUDY GUIDE AND PERSONAL APPLICATION

1. Are you looking forward to going to heaven? Why or why not?

2. Does a "home of righteousness" in heaven appeal to you, or do you feel at home in this world? In your own words, what would a "home of righteousness" look like?

3. How do you relate to the teaching to present the members of your body to Him while you are still present in this world? In what ways does that express the "new creation" in the midst of this world?

4. Do you see yourself wishing that God would invade this world with His justice the way Isaiah did? What would change in this world if God did that very thing?

5. Do you feel that we have missed God's heart for justice in the midst of our religious activities, just as did His people to whom Amos wrote? What things might we change in order to walk with God in the pursuit of justice in this world?

6. What does "kingdom living now" mean to us today? How can our attitudes more fully reflect the presence of God's Kingdom in this world?

7. Can you believe that we will actually live in a place where there will be no more death and no more night? How would you describe a place that would be called "heaven?" What else needs to happen there for it to be "heaven?"

8. Does everlasting worship appeal to you? Is that enough to fill your heart in heaven? What else would you desire?

REFLECTIONS, COMMITMENTS AND PRAYER

Heaven is the home of righteousness because the King of Righteousness is reigning there, the Lord Jesus. That is why there is no more death, and no more night. Everything there will be right. The worship will be more glorious than we can imagine. Our worship now is a reflection of that eternal worship. Spend some moments now worshiping the King of Righteousness, exalting Him in your heart and glorying in His commitment to what is just and right. Pray that God will give you His heart for justice, keeping you from losing what is most valuable in the midst of empty religious activities.

For it has been granted to you that for the sake of Christ you should not only believe in him but also suffer for his sake,

Philippians 1:29

7

The Fellowship of His Sufferings

As I read through 2 Peter 3 again and again, I was struck by how Peter repeats the phrase "looking forward." In fact, in verses twelve to fourteen, he repeats those words three times. One of Peter's primary commitments as he writes this letter under the inspiration of the Holy Spirit, is to turn our hearts from this world to heaven. He wants us to look toward what God prepared for us in His eternal glory rather than what He gave to us in the glory of this world. Paul also talks of this great truth in his first letter to the church at Corinth:

> But, as it is written, "What no eye has seen, nor ear heard, nor the heart of man imagined, what God has prepared for those who love him"— (1 Corinthians 2:9)

We so struggle with our lives rooted in this world rather than in Christ and His Kingdom. I battle this every day. I love my wife and my sons, I love my work, and I love my sports and hobbies.

When I travel, I am often vulnerable to depression. The travel and teaching schedule are part of that battle, and I struggle with being away from Karen. Another reason, however, is that I am away from those things I love in this world, the very things that I pursue for my comfort and enjoyment. Part of the very real spiritual warfare that I face from day to day is my love for this world. The Apostle John warned us about this very thing:

> Do not love the world or the things in the world. If anyone loves the world, the love of the Father is not in him. For all that is in the world—the desires of the flesh and the desires of the eyes and pride in possessions—is not from the Father but is from the world. (1 John 2:15-16)

This is a direct command from the Lord! When we love the world and the things in the world, we cannot love God at the same time. There is only room enough in our hearts for one passion. The nature of our passions is that the supreme passion of our heart consumes the lesser ones. It is an illusion to think that we can live functionally and fruitfully with competing passions. That is why John focuses immediately on our desires:

> And the world is passing away along with its desires, but whoever does the will of God abides forever. (1 John 2:17)

"The world is passing away," John says. We know that well from our study of 2 Peter 3. The elements will melt, the heavens will disappear, and the earth will be destroyed. So will our cravings, our boasts and our lusts. They will all pass away. What will remain forever? The person who does the will of God!

How Does God Teach Us to Look Forward?

What is the means that God uses to turn our focus and desires from this world toward heaven? It is suffering. The pain, affliction and loss that we bear in this life are tools in God's hands to draw the affections of our hearts from this world to Himself and the heavenly home He has prepared for us.

Karen's father died just a few months ago. We loved Dad so much. He was a wonderful father to Karen and her sisters and a father to me in every way as well. Mom and Dad had a beautiful marriage; they were married for sixty-three years. But when we remind Mom of the many glorious years that God gave them together, she says, "It wasn't nearly long enough!" We know that the deep pain Mom is bearing now is the "down side" of a long, loving, intimate friendship in marriage.

Mom is talking a lot about heaven now. She loves her Lord with whom she has walked for many years. Mom hungers for a home of righteousness. She knows that she will see her beloved husband and best friend in the resurrection when she will also see the face of her Lord. Mom is looking forward to heaven. God has used the sufferings of this present life to prepare her for the glory awaiting her in His presence.

As I mentioned earlier, I have had the joy of serving with Joni and Friends ministry. Joni describes her yearning for heaven in this way:

> I've been thinking about my heavenly home for years. Naturally, you can understand why: My earthly body doesn't work. That's one reason I dream about heaven all the time.[13]

Just as with Joni and Mom, God is using suffering in our lives to prepare us for heaven. In the resurrection Joni will receive her new body and in the resurrection Mom will be reunited with Dad. The pain of living in a body that has borne the brunt of sickness

---

[13]Joni Eareckson Tada, *Heaven: Your Real Home*, p. 33

and is in the process of dying does turn our eyes to look forward. The pain of separation from a loved one also causes us to look forward to heaven. It is God's grace in both instances that moves us to yearn for Him more and to love this world less.

CALLED TO SUFFER

Why do we suffer such pain, affliction and loss in this world? We suffer because that is God's calling for those He loves the most. Even His own Son suffered. We might think that God would protect His beloved Son from the pain of this hurting world. We are so accustomed to "self protection" that we would expect any person who had the opportunity to insulate himself from pain to do that very thing. God, however, put His Son into the very situation to experience the greatest pain that was ever known. He gave His only Son to bear all of the sin, rejection and pain of the whole world:

> Although he was a son, he learned obedience through what he suffered. (Hebrews 5:8)

Jesus, who was never disobedient, learned obedience. Through the sufferings of His life in this world, coming as the Lamb of God to take away our sin, Jesus learned that pattern of responsiveness that kept drawing Him back to His Father. We, too, are called to suffer. Paul taught the church at Philippi—these brothers and sisters he loved so deeply—about suffering for the sake of ministry:

> Only let your manner of life be worthy of the gospel of Christ, so that whether I come and see you or am absent, I may hear of you that you are standing firm in one spirit, with one mind striving side by side for the faith of the gospel, and not frightened in anything by your opponents. This is a clear sign to them of their de-

struction, but of your salvation, and that from God. (Philippians 1:27-28)

Paul spoke to them in the context of his own suffering. As he writes from a Roman jail, his brothers and sisters at Philippi are greatly concerned about him and about the gospel. He writes about returning to them and about their unity in the work of the gospel. Paul pictures their ministry as "contending for the faith." They need to know that they are in a battle, just as he is:

For it has been granted to you that for the sake of Christ you should not only believe in him but also suffer for his sake, engaged in the same conflict that you saw I had and now hear that I still have. (Philippians 1:29-30)

We are called to suffer. That ministry has been given to us in the name of Jesus. He not only calls us to salvation, but also to suffering. Later in this same letter, Paul gives the testimony of his own heart concerning his willingness to join Christ in His sufferings:

that I may know him and the power of his resurrection, and may share his sufferings, becoming like him in his death, that by any means possible I may attain the resurrection from the dead. (Philippians 3:10-11)

This is the cry of a servant passionately in love with His master. The deepest desire of Paul's heart was to know Christ. Paul wanted to know His Lord fully, sharing life and ministry with Him on every level. He wanted to experience His power from day to day at every point of need and opportunity. He also wanted to join the fellowship of Jesus' sufferings. In Paul's understanding, this was all part of sharing in the hope of the resurrection.

WILL WE SUFFER WRATH?

The theology that teaches us that we do not need to prepare to suffer, because God promises to "whisk His Church away" before the suffering and pain of this world become terrible in "the last days," leads to a very soft and weak Church in many parts of the world, particularly in the developed nations. Paul did talk about us not being "destined for wrath" in his first letter to the church at Thessalonica:

> For God has not destined us for wrath, but to obtain salvation through our Lord Jesus Christ, (1 Thessalonians 5:9)

What is the wrath that Paul is talking about here? It is the same wrath that Peter is describing in 2 Peter 3, the wrath of The Day of The Lord, where everything will be destroyed in Christ's Second Coming. Then the elements will melt, the heavens will disappear, and the earth will be laid bare on that day of judgment when the Father will destroy the ungodly. We will escape that wrath because of our faith in Christ and the blood of His righteousness, but we will not escape suffering in this world. We are called to suffer:

> Indeed, all who desire to live a godly life in Christ Jesus will be persecuted, (2 Timothy 3:12)

We must know that each of us will suffer as believers if we would endure in life and ministry in this evil and pain-filled world. If we do not submit to the truth of the Scriptures and the reality of God's call on the lives of His people, we will continually be reconstructing our theology to fit our circumstances and conforming our image of God to fit our dreams for life and our desires for comfort.

Jesus is brutally honest with those He calls to follow Him. Unlike many who would develop a following in this world and build a kingdom of their own, Christ calls His followers to lay down their lives for a Kingdom that will last forever. The depth of Jesus' openness with His disciples is almost beyond belief. We can hardly imagine anyone following Him when He reveals the reality of a disciple's future like this:

> Brother will deliver brother over to death, and the father his child, and children will rise against parents and have them put to death, (Matthew 10:21)

What would be the most painful rejection of all? What could possibly confront us in life and ministry that would cause us to cry out, "That is more than I can handle? Who could possibly pay such a price?" We could understand rejection in this world, and even prepare for it, if we have the love and support of our families. Can you imagine being betrayed by a family member, a betrayal resulting in our death? Can we conceive of our own children putting us to death because of the gospel? This has happened many times throughout Church history:

> and you will be hated by all for my name's sake. But the one who endures to the end will be saved. (Matthew 10:22)

Sometimes it will seem that we are the objects of hatred by all those around us. Will we identify with the name of Jesus to that degree? How do we respond in those times? We hold on to God, focus on our Father's eyes and keep walking. We remind our selves that the suffering of these present times is nothing compared to the glory that will be revealed in us and for us. God is preparing an eternal glory for us that will far surpass the afflictions that we are bearing now. Earlier we looked at this powerful truth in our study of Romans 8 and 2 Corinthians 4:

173

For I consider that the sufferings of this present time are not worth comparing with the glory that is to be revealed to us. (Romans 8:18)

FILLING UP WHAT IS LACKING

The Apostle Paul made one of the most fascinating comments concerning his sufferings, and ours, in his letter to the church at Colossae:

Now I rejoice in my sufferings for your sake, and in my flesh I am filling up what is lacking in Christ's afflictions for the sake of his body, that is, the church, (Colossians 1:24)

What could possibly be lacking in Christ's afflictions? Didn't He say from the cross, just before He released His life to His Father, "It is finished" (John 19:30)? What could be left undone that Paul, or you and I could complete?

The Scriptures are filled with the graphic descriptions of our Lord's suffering. The prophet Isaiah saw it clearly some seven hundred years before Jesus died on the Cross:

He was despised and rejected by men; a man of sorrows, and acquainted with grief; and as one from whom men hide their faces he was despised, and we esteemed him not. (Isaiah 53:3)

Jesus was a man of sorrows and familiar with suffering. The Lord of glory was rejected and despised. Isaiah continues to describe how Jesus picked up our sickness and our weakness, that He was pierced and crushed for our sins. Jesus' punishment, as He bore the wrath of a holy God, brought us peace and healing:

Surely he has borne our griefs and carried our sorrows; yet we esteemed him stricken, smitten by God, and afflicted. (Isaiah 53:4)

No matter how graphically the Scriptures describe our Lord's suffering, our minds and our hearts are far too small and too limited to even begin to grasp the realities of the words we read. The agony and confusion of being forsaken by His Father, the weight of sin from every person who has ever lived, the rejection of even His closest friends, the pain of the crucifixion are all beyond our comprehension.

What could possibly be lacking? So complete was His sacrifice that our God of holiness and righteousness was satisfied. Of course, there is no lack in the sufficiency of the atonement. Jesus paid for our sins fully at the cross. What Paul is referring to in Colossians 1:24 is the unfinished work of Jesus' sufferings. His sufferings are not finished in the sense that they are still going on.

When our Lord came to earth, the Father gave Him a physical body. That physical body bore the suffering and pain of this temporal world and the pain of our sin. Jesus still has a physical body; it is His Church. His Body is still suffering. God calls us to participate in the sufferings of His Son and to bring to completion the afflictions of His body.

THE PRICE OF THE CROSS

Jesus told His disciples at the very beginning of His call on their hearts that identifying with Him would cost them their lives. As He gave them the Beatitudes, Christ warned them that to own the Kingdom meant a willingness to suffer persecution:

> Blessed are those who are persecuted for righteousness' sake, for theirs is the kingdom of heaven. (Matthew 5:10)

We do not often link the blessing of God with the pain of our lives. Mostly, we think of God's "blessings" as He pours the good things of His hand into our careers, our families, our finances, and our health. Jesus is teaching us to seek the blessing of the Father—His stamp of approval and eternal affirmation—in the evil, rejection and pain that come from following Him:

> Blessed are you when others revile you and persecute you and utter all kinds of evil against you falsely on my account. Rejoice and be glad, for your reward is great in heaven, for so they persecuted the prophets who were before you. (Matthew 5:11-12)

This message was given again and again as Jesus sought disciples. He warned them continually that the way of the cross was not His call alone; it was their call as well. Luke records the words of the Lord Jesus this way:

> Now great crowds accompanied him, and he turned and said to them, "If anyone comes to me and does not hate his own father and mother and wife and children and brothers and sisters, yes, and even his own life, he cannot be my disciple." (Luke 14:25-26)

All of our relationships must be submitted to Christ if we would follow Him. The gospel might very well cost us the love of our parents or our children or our marriage partner. It will surely cost us our own lives. This undoubtedly was not the message the crowds had come to hear:

> Whoever does not bear his own cross and come after me cannot be my disciple. (Luke 14:27)

The cross has always been a symbol of suffering and death. There was no mistaking the message the multitudes were hearing. Following Jesus will cost our lives. That may come at the end of a sword, or a gun, it may be in a lonely prison, it may be seen in an area of obedience that is expensive to our secret loves or to our pride. Following Christ may cost us our most precious relationships. It will, without question, cost us our lives. It might mean loneliness, painful obedience, loss, or even death. In some way, at some time, for every one of us, being a disciple of Jesus will mean laying down our life.

THE FIFTH SPARROW

When we face the cross, we need to see ourselves through our Father's eyes. As those who would destroy us surround us, we must remember that we are valuable to the God who has called us to serve Him. We are precious in His sight. When Jesus prepared His disciples for the suffering that would be theirs as they followed Him, He told them not to fear those who could only destroy their bodies, but to fear God. Then He told them this wonderful truth:

> Are not two sparrows sold for a penny? And not one of them will fall to the ground apart from your Father. But even the hairs of your head are all numbered. (Matthew 10:29-30)

Even sparrows are precious to their creator. Not one falls to the ground without His knowledge. Pastor Bill Johnson, who shepherded our church for over thirty years, loved to tell the story of "the fifth sparrow." His reference comes from the companion Scripture to this very teaching in the book of Luke:

> Are not five sparrows sold for two pennies? And not one of them is forgotten before God. Why, even the hairs of your head are all numbered. Fear not; you are of more value than many sparrows. (Luke 12:6-7)

Two sparrows are sold for one penny. Five sparrows for two pennies. What is that fifth sparrow worth? Nothing in the eyes of this world; in fact, it is just a "throw in" on the deal! But that sparrow is valuable to God; He does not forget it. He will not forget us in our suffering. God is there with us each moment as we take up our cross and follow Him.

FAITH THAT CONQUERS: FAITH THAT TRIUMPHS

The writer to the Hebrews tells us more about the price of the cross in following Jesus. He spent almost an entire chapter affirming those who pursued God with a whole heart of faith. In chapter eleven, he talked about the heroes of the past who trusted in the Lord in situations where human reasoning might lead them in a completely different direction. God gave them the faith that made them strong, vessels for His glory, and examples for you and me. Toward the end of that great chapter, the writer begins to summarize some of those models of faith:

> And what more shall I say? For time would fail me to tell of Gideon, Barak, Samson, Jephthah, of David and Samuel and the prophets—who through faith conquered kingdoms, enforced justice, obtained promises, stopped the mouths of lions, (Hebrews 11:32-33)

When we look at these names, we remember the stories of their lives from the Old Testament. They were people of extraordinary faith because they placed their hope in a great God. In fact, they were all very ordinary people who were made out of dust just like us. But through even a small amount of faith in a great and powerful God they conquered, brought justice and faced down lions:

> quenched the power of fire, escaped the edge of the sword, were made strong out of weakness, became mighty in war, put foreign armies to flight. Women received back their dead by resurrection. Some were tortured, refusing to accept release, so that they might rise again to a better life. (Hebrews 11:34-35)

The historical record is in the Word of God. We can actually read the stories of these incredible men and women. They were strong and faithful as they confronted the sword and the flames. In their own weakness, they saw God's strength and His great victories. Some saw even resurrections of their loved ones, and others sought a better resurrection than can be experienced in this physical world. They were willing to suffer in order to share in Christ's resurrection:

> Others suffered mocking and flogging, and even chains and imprisonment. They were stoned, they were sawn in two, they were killed with the sword. They went about in skins of sheep and goats, destitute, afflicted, mistreated— (Hebrews 11:36-37)

This list is quite different from the one we read a moment ago. Those in the previous list walked in incredible power and victory. The writer describes now a completely different fruit of faithfulness. This second group of heroes did not rout the foreign armies; rather, they were routed in the eyes of this world. They experienced torture, they were mocked and ridiculed; they were beaten and imprisoned.

We can hardly grasp the horror of what the writer is setting before us. These were God's own chosen people. They trusted in Him. How could He allow this to happen to His most faithful children? But here it is. They were not only stoned; some were actually sawn in two. They faced the sword with courage, they possessed only the skins of animals, and they were penniless and persecuted:

> of whom the world was not worthy—wandering about in deserts and mountains, and in dens and caves of the earth. (Hebrews 11:38)

These precious, faithful servants of our Lord owned no dwelling in this world. They wandered and lived in caves. The people of this world laughed at them, but this world was not worthy even of their presence. God's people had no value in the eyes of their enemies, but they were of great worth in His sight:

> And all these, though commended through their faith, did not receive what was promised, (Hebrews 11:39)

We read here about two very different responses to faith. We have seen amazing victories and terrible suffering. Were some of these brothers and sisters lacking in their faith? If those who were persecuted had just a little more faith, could they also have experienced the victories? No! It is the same faith and the same loving and powerful God, and it is the same glory revealed. God sovereignly designed the circumstances and the lives of His people in order to display His glory in them. Everyone in this list was commended for his faith, not in the eyes of this world but in the eyes of their Father.

SUFFERING REVEALS THE GLORY OF GOD

Even though the brothers and sisters that we read about in Hebrews 11 were strongly affirmed for their faith, the writer tells us that they did not receive what was promised. For each of them, their faith pointed to both a savior and a heavenly Kingdom. We have that savior in Jesus, and we have inherited the Kingdom which they saw only at a distance. Their faith has been brought to completion in our experience, and together we share in the fulfillment of God's eternal plan:

> since God had provided something better for us, that apart from us they should not be made perfect. (Hebrews 11:40)

We share in the fullness of God's great eternal plan only together with the saints who have gone before us. We are one with them in the faith. The same is true of our brothers and sisters that are serving the Lord in hurting places around the world. We are one with them as well. In fact, the writer to the Hebrews talks later in his letter about remembering and identifying with members of the Body of Christ who are suffering and imprisoned:

> Remember those who are in prison, as though in prison with them, and those who are mistreated, since you also are in the body. (Hebrews 13:3)

A few years ago, I was in Shanghai, China, with my coworkers Craig Parro and Henry Chua. We were walking down a street in Shanghai at 10:00 p.m. on one of our first evenings there. As we passed a church, Henry suggested that we see if the pastor was still there. Perhaps he would like to meet us and visit for a few minutes. I said, "We can't disturb him this late in the evening, Henry." But Henry was sure the pastor would love nothing more than to visit with us at this late hour!

We rang the bell at the gate, and the caretaker answered the door. Yes, the pastor was still awake, and yes, he would love to meet his brothers from America! We waited for a few moments, and then the pastor came out. Henry translated for us as we began to talk with one another. This pastor was so gracious and warm. He seemed to be about seventy years of age.

As we visited with pastors in China, we were always curious to know what happened to them and their church during the "Cultural Revolution." From 1966 until about 1976, there was chaos in the land of China. The universities were closed. The political leaders abdicated their responsibility and gave unhindered freedom to the youth and to all who reacted to the systems of the past. In that chaos and rebellion, the cultures of business, education and religion were destroyed. Anyone who was perceived to possess wealth, own a business, hold a position of authority or a place of leadership in either the religious or educational community was viewed with suspicion.

The pastor told us how his church was closed and turned into a "reeducation center" for Chinese youth. He was captured and beaten and then paraded through the streets wearing a "dunce cap." Then he was sent out to the far provinces of China to work in the fields. He was separated from his family, confused and alone. His exile to hard labor lasted until the revolution was over.

The hardship of those years of revolution caused many of the pastors to recant their beliefs and leave the ministry. Many of the leaders in the churches were political appointees and did not have a genuine call of God on their lives. Many of these pastors did not endure the suffering of those years. Those who did endure were strong and faithful brothers and sisters, just like the ones remembered in Hebrews 11.

The pastor that we visited that night did endure. After the Cultural Revolution was over, he returned to Shanghai and his church. Faithfully, he began to minister to his people once again as the government had allowed his church to reopen. God blessed his ministry and the church grew significantly. We talked further about God's goodness and His faithfulness over those painful years.

We stood there at the back of this faithful pastor's church, sharing together about the amazing work of God in his beloved nation. I said to him, "It must fill you with incredible joy to be able to come back to your own church and to pastor your people once again. You must be in awe of the great work God is doing as He is building His Church in China."

I stood there in the presence of this man "of whom the world was not worthy," waiting for him to respond to my comments. He wanted to respond but he was weeping. Finally, I said, "He is the

Lord of the harvest, isn't He." After a moment, he responded, "Yes," he said, "even in the desert, He is Lord of the harvest."

SUFFERING DEVELOPS MINISTRY

One of the ways that God glorifies Himself in suffering is that He uses it to develop ministry in our lives. One of the glorious truths of the Scriptures is that our sovereign God is able to use the very things that would destroy us as tools in His hands to make us the people He called us to be. Paul talks about this very thing in the beginning of his second letter to the church at Corinth:

> Blessed be the God and Father of our Lord Jesus Christ, the Father of mercies and God of all comfort, (2 Corinthians 1:3)

This is my favorite description of God found anywhere in His Word. He is "the Father of mercies, the God of all comfort." There is no compassion found anywhere in this world except for what comes from the heart of our Father. Any mercy that is ever given or received has only one source—the heart of God:

> who comforts us in all our affliction, so that we may be able to comfort those who are in any affliction, with the comfort with which we ourselves are comforted by God. (2 Corinthians 1:4)

This statement stretches our view of God and the way He works. When we face troubles, God comforts us. In our suffering, our Father meets us with His mercy and heals our hearts. He brings us the comfort of His love. But God has a bigger view for our suffering and His comfort than just the effects of His compassion on our own lives. He desires for us to give His heart to others who are hurting. We are living in a pain-filled world where those around us are bearing more pain than anyone can possibly han-

183

dle. Our Father desires that we reach out to them with the mercy that comes from Him alone. He wants that comfort to overflow:

> For as we share abundantly in Christ's sufferings, so through Christ we share abundantly in comfort too. (2 Corinthians 1:5)

We see here, once again, that truth from the Scriptures which calls us to share in Christ's sufferings. We "share abundantly" in the sufferings of our Lord." This is a vivid picture of how God develops ministry in us. The reservoir of our hearts is filled with the compassion and comfort which come from God's heart as He allows us to go through suffering, and then He brings us to hurting people so that we can give to them the comfort God gave to us when we were hurting. We share in Christ's sufferings as we share vicariously the sufferings of our brothers and sisters in the Body of Christ, and they share in His comfort through the love we bring to them.

SUFFERING LEADS US TO HOLINESS

The Apostle Peter also taught us about sharing in the sufferings of Christ. He wrote to brothers and sisters who were in the midst of suffering almost beyond belief, as we will see later in this chapter. In his letter, he tells us one of the primary purposes for which God designed suffering. It is part of His process for the Christian life and ministry because suffering brings us to holiness:

> Since therefore Christ suffered in the flesh, arm yourselves with the same way of thinking, for whoever has suffered in the flesh has ceased from sin, (1 Peter 4:1)

With Christ as our model, Peter calls us to "arm ourselves with the same attitude." The attitude he is describing is that of submission so clearly seen in Jesus. Why do we submit to suffering? Because suffering deals with the sin in our lives:

so as to live for the rest of the time in the flesh no longer for human passions but for the will of God. (1 Peter 4:2)

Peter said that when we suffer in our bodies as Jesus did, God does an amazing work within us. He brings us to the place where we live the rest of our days on this earth in order to fulfill His will, rather than living for our own desires. Believers who understand the Scriptures welcome the Father's process in their lives, even when it is painful:

The time that is past suffices for doing what the Gentiles want to do, living in sensuality, passions, drunkenness, orgies, drinking parties, and lawless idolatry. With respect to this they are surprised when you do not join them in the same flood of debauchery, and they malign you; (1 Peter 4:3-4)

All of our past, before we came to know Christ, was spent in the pursuit of this world's lifestyle. Your past, Peter says, held plenty of time for that. Even your friends are surprised that you do not run with them anymore into the emptiness of this world, and they verbally abuse you:

but they will give account to him who is ready to judge the living and the dead. For this is why the gospel was preached even to those who are dead, that though judged in the flesh the way people are, they might live in the spirit the way God does. (1 Peter 4:5-6)

Every man and woman who has ever lived will give an account of their lives to the Lord. If we allow our lives to be dissipated into nothingness here in this world, we are responsible before Him for that. The gospel has been preached even to those who came before us so that, as Peter says, they might experience man's judgment in their bodies but God's will in their spirits:

The Day of the Lord!

> The end of all things is at hand; therefore be self-controlled and sober-minded for the sake of your prayers. (1 Peter 4:7)

We live only for the fulfillment of God's will in this world because the time is near for all things to be culminated in Christ. Therefore Peter sets before us one of his most consistent exhortations: think soundly and be holy in order to pray, participating with the Father in the fulfillment of the times. After he calls us to love one another, Peter returns to the theme of suffering:

> Beloved, do not be surprised at the fiery trial when it comes upon you to test you, as though something strange were happening to you. But rejoice insofar as you share Christ's sufferings, that you may also rejoice and be glad when his glory is revealed. (1 Peter 4:12-13)

Like Peter's readers in the first century, we should never be surprised at the suffering we experience. It is not strange that we suffer as God's children for that is the process He chose for us, just as He did His own Son. We suffer because God called us to participate in the sufferings of Jesus, and when we suffer, we share in His joy.

Suffering leads us to holiness. It is the process in which we share with our Lord on an intimate level. God also uses this process to free us from sin in order that we might serve Him.

I have experienced that in my own life. Some years ago, I developed attitudes toward my wife that were less than God would have them be and priorities that were out of order. I allowed myself to fall into patterns and desires that were not holy. Through a car accident and several months of recovery, and a resulting physical vulnerability that God allowed, I have seen my faithful, loving Father turn my heart from this world toward His Kingdom and toward holiness in His eyes. His process is full of grace, and glory:

186

And after you have suffered a little while, the God of all grace, who has called you to his eternal glory in Christ, will himself restore, confirm, strengthen, and establish you. To him be the dominion forever and ever. Amen. (1 Peter 5:10-11)

Isn't this an incredible hope? God is with us at every point of suffering; and even though our pain might seem endless in our eyes, it is a brief time in our Father's eyes. He promises to restore us from our broken condition and in the process build His strength into us. He will keep our hearts steadfast by His grace and lift our hearts to worship Him.

GOD GIVES HIS LIFE AWAY AS WE DIE

Paul comes back to the theme of God using suffering to develop ministry later in his second Corinthian letter. He teaches us that God placed the treasure of His Son's life in us, a vessel of clay:

But we have this treasure in jars of clay, to show that the surpassing power belongs to God and not to us. (2 Corinthians 4:7)

God desires to be the only explanation for our lives and ministries. His supreme commitment is to His own glory, even as He calls us to lay down our lives. God wants to put His glory on display through the circumstances we face and the afflictions that we bear. He makes it clear, however, that His presence is with us in every circumstance and relationship:

We are afflicted in every way, but not crushed; perplexed, but not driven to despair; persecuted, but not forsaken; struck down, but not destroyed; (2 Corinthians 4:8-9)

At every point of affliction and confusion, God is there with us. When we are persecuted, He is present. When we are losing heart, God reminds us of His faithfulness, and He lifts our hearts with encouragement. He holds us and does not allow us to be destroyed:

> always carrying in the body the death of Jesus, so that the life of Jesus may also be manifested in our bodies. (2 Corinthians 4:10)

When we talk about "the fellowship of His sufferings," it is hard to grasp the intimacy of that experience. How closely we identify with and share the pain involved in the afflictions borne in the Body of Christ! If there is any doubt, Paul makes it crystal clear. We are carrying in our bodies the death of Jesus. This is the way God has designed His life to be revealed in us:

> For we who live are always being given over to death for Jesus' sake, so that the life of Jesus also may be manifested in our mortal flesh. So death is at work in us, but life in you. (2 Corinthians 4:11,12)

This "life and death" identification with Jesus is not only because we bear His name and His reproach, it is because of God's design and purpose. He brings us into situations where we die in order that His life might be revealed, even released through us. While death is working in us, God is pouring out His life through us to those around us for His glory. Elisabeth Elliot talked about this Scripture in this way:

> Do the ways of God seem strange to some that are honestly seeking only to be good and faithful servants? There are stormy winds, long, silent years of stress, deaths to be died. The One we serve has not left us without inside information as to the why. All who would bring souls to God and multiply His kingdom must do so through surrender and sacrifice. This is what loving God means, a continual offering, a pure readiness to give oneself away, a happy obedi-

ence. There is no question of "But what about me?" for the motivation is love. All interests, all impulses, all energies are subjugated to that supreme passion, ..."[14]

There is no question that following Jesus will mean giving up our lives. That is the price of the Cross. God designed life and ministry so that His life is released in the process of our dying.

SUFFERING CONFORMS US TO THE IMAGE OF CHRIST

The Apostle James talked about suffering in his letter as well. He was writing to his Jewish brothers and sisters who had believed in Christ and were now dispersed among the surrounding nations:

> Count it all joy, my brothers, when you meet trials of various kinds, for you know that the testing of your faith produces steadfastness. (James 1:2-3)

The believers to whom James is writing were in the midst of terrible persecutions. That is why he talks of many kinds of trials. He desires, though, to give them a larger perspective on their life experiences, just as Paul does when he teaches us about the eternal weight of glory that God is preparing for us in the midst of our momentary afflictions. James tells us that God is in the process with us, and He is using these afflictions to enable us to endure. He is testing our faith:

> And let steadfastness have its full effect, that you may be perfect and complete, lacking in nothing. (James 1:4)

---

[14]Elisabeth Elliot, *A Path Through Suffering*, (Ann Arbor, MI: Servant Publications, 1990), p. 101.

As we persevere in the battles, the trials and the afflictions, God is bringing us to maturity in His Son. When we endure, we participate with God in His process in our lives. His desire is to build into us the character qualities of Christ, and suffering is a tool in His hand to bring that process to completion. We, too, need to keep the "big picture" in view. There is a crown waiting for us at the end of God's faithful, loving process:

> Blessed is the man who perseveres under trial, because when he has stood the test, he will receive the crown of life that God has promised to those who love him. (James 1:12)

"I Wouldn't Change a Thing"

Paul taught the church at Rome about these same truths. He begins this time of teaching with the justification that is ours before a holy God through the faith we placed in His Son and the peace which flows from it:

> Therefore, since we have been justified by faith, we have peace with God through our Lord Jesus Christ. Through him we have also obtained access by faith into this grace in which we stand, and we rejoice in hope of the glory of God. (Romans 5:1-2)

How wonderful it is to know that the grace of God is not only the means to our salvation, it actually becomes the environment for our lives! We stand right now in the grace of God. When Paul talks again about the relationship between our joy, our hope and God's glory, we remember once more the eternal weight of glory awaiting us:

> More than that, we rejoice in our sufferings, knowing that suffering produces endurance, and endurance produces character, and character produces hope, (Romans 5:3-4)

We find joy even in our sufferings, Paul says, not because we enjoy pain but because we know that God uses the sufferings to develop endurance. As we hold onto God and continue to walk with Him, He conforms us ever more to the image of His Son. The more we become like Jesus, the more God fills us with hope. Then Paul sets before us a truth that can transform our hearts:

> and hope does not put us to shame, because God's love has been poured into our hearts through the Holy Spirit who has been given to us. (Romans 5:5)

Hope does not disappoint us, Paul says. It does not disappoint because God is pouring out His love into our lives through His Holy Spirit. If we can correlate this truth to his teaching in 2 Corinthians 1, we will remember that Paul uses similar language concerning our sufferings. The sufferings of this world flow into our lives, but God's love flows even more fully. That is how He fills us with hope.

This is a truth from the heart of God that can transform our lives. This means that we can say to a cancer patient, a hurting parent, a crushed marriage partner, and a pastor who has lost heart, "Place your hope in God, and you will not be disappointed." All of these people might very well be disappointed with God along the way, but at the end of the process, they will not be disappointed with God nor with what He has done in their lives.

Do you realize what this means to us? This incredible truth tells us that on the day we stand before God's glorious throne and we think of all that God did in all of our days, we will look into our Father's eyes and say, "I wouldn't change a thing." No one who places their hope in God will be disappointed.

CLIMBING "HILL DIFFICULTY"

In John Piper's wonderful book *The Hidden Smile of God*, he uses John Bunyan, the author of *Pilgrim's Progress*, as an illustration of the suffering that produces character and endurance. Bunyan not only wrote about suffering, he experienced it while imprisoned in England for twelve years.

In describing the hero of *Pilgrim's Progress*, the man named Christian moving toward the Celestial City, he confronts "Hill Difficulty." Piper tells us this about the nature of suffering:

> Bunyan's life and labor call us to live like Pilgrim on the way to the Celestial City. His suffering and his story summon us, in the prosperous and pleasure-addicted West, to see the Christian life in a radically different way than we ordinarily do. There is a great gulf between the Christianity that wrestles with whether to worship at the cost of imprisonment and death, and the Christianity that wrestles with whether the kids should play soccer on Sunday morning. The full title of *The Pilgrim's Progress* shows the essence of the pilgrim path: "The Pilgrim's Progress from this World, to that Which is to Come: Delivered under the Similitude of a Dream wherein Is Discovered, the Manner of His Setting out, his Dangerous Journey, and Safe Arrival at the Desired Country." For Bunyan, in fact and fiction, the Christian life is a "Dangerous Journey."

> The narrow way leads from the Wicket Gate to the Hill Difficulty.
> The narrow way lay right up the hill, and the name of the going up the side of the hill is called *Difficulty*. Christian now went to the Spring, and drank thereof, to refresh himself (Isaiah 49:10), and then began to go up the Hill saying,

The Hill, though high, I covet to ascend,
The Difficulty will not me offend;
For I perceive the Way to life lies here.
Come, pluck up Heart, let's neither faint nor fear;
Better, though difficult, the Right Way to go,
Than wrong, though easy, where the End is Woe.

This is the Christian life for Bunyan—experienced in prison and explained in parables. But we modern, western Christians have come to see safety and ease as a right. We move away from bad neighborhoods. We leave hard relationships. We don't go to dangerous, unreached people groups.

Bunyan reckons us to listen to Jesus and his apostles again. Jesus never called us to a life of safety, nor even to a fair fight. "Lambs in the midst of wolves" is the way he describes our sending (Luke 10:3).[15]

HIS GRACE IS SUFFICIENT

Just as James and Paul write to us about the relationship between suffering, hope and grace, the Apostle Peter does as well. In his letter, Peter writes about the believers scattered among the nations because of persecutions. He writes to lift their eyes to see God exalted above, but intimately involved with them in their sufferings:

> Blessed be the God and Father of our Lord Jesus Christ! According to his great mercy, he has caused us to be born again to a living hope through the resurrection of Jesus Christ from the dead, (1 Peter 1:3)

---

[15]John Piper, *The Hidden Smile of God*, (Wheaton, IL: Crossway Books, 2001), pp. 164-165.

The brothers and sisters to whom Peter is writing lost almost everything. They had lost family members, businesses, bank accounts, and homes. Peter tells them that they still have a hope that is alive, one that is not limited to this world in which they live:

> to an inheritance that is imperishable, undefiled, and unfading, kept in heaven for you, (1 Peter 1:4)

They not only have hope, they also have an inheritance that will not be consumed in this life. It will be waiting for them in heaven when they get there:

> who by God's power are being guarded through faith for a salvation ready to be revealed in the last time. (1 Peter 1:5)

Having a hope that is alive and an inheritance that is imperishable is a truth that lifts the hearts of hurting brothers and sisters. Even in the midst of pain, they can worship Him. While they remain in this world of afflictions, they live protected by the power of God. Not for even one moment, in any situation, in any relationship, even in these devastating persecutions, have they been outside of God's protection. His power is their shield and His presence their hope.

So it is for you and me. We share a hope that is alive. We possess an inheritance that is imperishable. We live protected by His power every moment of our lives, even as our Father prepares us in costly ways to meet the Bridegroom.

This was the experience of Thomas Hauker who gave his life for the sake of the gospel in England in 1555:

> "Thomas," his friend lowered his voice so as not to be heard by the guard. "I have to ask you this favor. I need to know if what the others say about the grace of God is true. Tomorrow, when they burn you at the

stake, if the pain is tolerable and your mind is still at peace, lift your hands above your head. Do it right before you die. Thomas, I *have* to know."

Thomas Hauker whispered to his friend, "I will."

The next morning Hauker was bound to the stake and the fire was lit. The fire burned a long time, but Hauker remained motionless. His skin was burnt to a crisp and his fingers were gone. Everyone watching supposed he was dead. Suddenly, miraculously, Hauker lifted his hands, still on fire, over his head. He reached them up to the living God, and then with great rejoicing, clapped them together three times. The people there broke into shouts of praise and applause. Hauker's friend had his answer.[16]

How could Thomas Hauker endure such suffering with amazing joy? Because Hauker believed, with the Apostle Paul and with countless saints throughout history, that God keeps His promises.

For I consider that the sufferings of this present time are not worth comparing with the glory that is to be revealed to us. (Romans 8:18)

GROUP STUDY GUIDE
AND PERSONAL APPLICATION

1. When you learn that God has called you to suffer for His sake, how does that affect your view of Him?

2. What has God used in your life to turn your eyes and your heart to look forward to heaven?

---

[16]d.c. Talk, *Jesus Freaks: dc Talk and The Voice of the Martyrs, Stories of those who stood for Jesus: the ultimate Jesus Freaks,* (Tulsa, OK: Albury Publishing, 1999), p. 144.

3. Paul told Timothy that everyone who desires to live a godly life will suffer persecution. How has persecution touched your life?

4. How does the thought of "filling up what is lacking" in Christ's afflictions strike you? Does it bring you joy to share with Him so intimately, or anger at the pain you must face in His name?

5. What has it meant in your life to "take up the cross" and follow Jesus?

6. Does the teaching on the "fifth sparrow" bring comfort to your heart? What difference has it made in your life to see yourself through the eyes of God?

7. As you look back over your life, and then you look at Hebrews 12:32-38, which of those two results of faith have you most experienced? Have you questioned the depth of your faith in either case?

8. When you look at God's process of developing His heart of compassion within us in the process of suffering, as it is revealed in 2 Corinthians 1:3-5, do you feel that the prize is worth the pain?

9. As you look over your life experiences now, can you imagine standing before the throne of God and saying, "I wouldn't change a thing?"

10. Thinking back on John Piper's comment on the difference between "the Christianity that wrestles with whether to worship at the cost of imprisonment and death, and the Christianity that wrestles with whether the kids should play soccer on Sunday morning," what comes to your mind about our views of suffering in the developing nations?

11. Knowing what you know about suffering, would you encourage your children to go to the mission field? Why, or why not?

REFLECTIONS, COMMITMENTS AND PRAYER

Perhaps you, like me, are confronted with the softness of your commitment to the cross, whatever the cost, as you study these Scriptures. Confess that to the Lord with me. Ask God to build into you His view of life and ministry, which includes pain and suffering. Pray that He will give you the strength to endure with Him in whatever process He allows in your life and to give you His joy along the way as well. Pray for the Church in the developed nations, too, that God will strengthen us and enable us to confront the cross, and carry it wherever He leads.

And count the patience of our Lord as salvation, just as our beloved brother Paul also wrote to you according to the wisdom given him,

2 Peter 3:15

8

Come and Join the Party!

Earlier in our study, we looked at Peter's admonition concerning God's timing in The Day of the Lord. The scoffers said that it had been so long since Jesus ascended to the Father and promised to return, and nothing has changed. Why should we continue to place any confidence in His coming? Peter responded with the historical record of God's faithfulness to His Word. The Word of God created the heavens and the earth. By the same Word, the Flood came upon this earth. We can be confident that God will keep His promise in the return of His Son.

Peter went on to teach us the reason it had been so long between Christ's promise and His return. God is not slow but patient. He desires all to come to repentance. God is patiently waiting for our family members, our neighbors, our coworkers and the nations to repent and to place their faith in His Son. He returns to that theme later in the chapter, as he describes for us once again the glorious heart of God:

> And count the patience of our Lord as salvation, just as our beloved brother Paul also wrote to you according to the wisdom given him, (2 Peter 3:15)

As we seek to know God's purposes in preparing us to meet the Bridegroom, it is wise to look at the themes repeated in the Apostle Peter's letter to us. We saw it in our last chapter, as he called us again and again to "look forward." Our Father wants us to share His eternal focus as He is preparing for the new heavens and the new earth. He is turning our eyes from this world to heaven and His eternal Kingdom.

We see another repetition in Peter's teaching here. For the second time, he tells us that God is patient. But this time he adds that God's patience means salvation. He is waiting to fulfill time in The Day of the Lord so that more people can be saved. Our Father wants us to share His heart, and He wants us to share His joy.

THE SINNERS AND THE MUTTERERS

Luke records for us a series of three parables in the fifteenth chapter of his book. He begins the parables by setting the scene for the teaching. There is a gathering of tax collectors, sinners, Pharisees, and teachers of the law:

> Now the tax collectors and sinners were all drawing near to hear him. And the Pharisees and the scribes grumbled, saying, "This man receives sinners and eats with them." (Luke 15:1-2)

What a graphic picture that is! The sinners are gathering around Jesus, eager to receive His teaching and the religious leaders are muttering. Why are they muttering? Because Jesus welcomes sinners! Jesus eats with sinners. I know that you and I are grateful that Jesus welcomes and fellowships with sinners because that is all of the reason that we know Him.

Why are the religious leaders of God's people surprised that Jesus welcomes the broken people of this world into His presence? Because they would never do that! The Pharisees and the teachers of the law see themselves so far above these poor souls who cannot produce a life of righteousness. It is clear that they do not see themselves through the eyes of God.

THE LOST SHEEP

Jesus begins now to tell His first story. It is about sheep and a shepherd. The religious leaders as well as the sinners can relate to this parable because the scene is found everywhere in their culture:

> So he told them this parable: "What man of you, having a hundred sheep, if he has lost one of them, does not leave the ninety-nine in the open country, and go after the one that is lost, until he finds it?" (Luke 15:3-4)

The audience is visualizing the scene. They know the shepherd who owns the one hundred sheep. It breaks the heart of the shepherd if one of his sheep is lost, not only because of the value of the sheep but because the shepherd genuinely loves the sheep. He begins to search, and he looks everywhere until he finds his sheep that has gone astray. What happens when he finds it?:

> And when he has found it, he lays it on his shoulders, rejoicing. And when he comes home, he calls together his friends and his neighbors, saying to them, "Rejoice with me, for I have found my sheep that was lost." (Luke 15:5-6)

When the shepherd finds his lost sheep, his heart is filled with joy. He puts the sheep on his shoulders and carries it home. This is the story of my life. I was a lost and broken person when the Shepherd found me, put me on His shoulders and carried me home. And my life has never been the same!

The Shepherd then calls all of his friends and neighbors to join him in a time of celebration. They rejoice together at his good fortune in finding the sheep that was lost:

> Just so, I tell you, there will be more joy in heaven over one sinner who repents than over ninety-nine righteous persons who need no repentance. (Luke 15:7)

Jesus makes His point clear. The Pharisees and teachers of the Law see no need in their hearts to repent as they believe that their own righteousness is sufficient to please a holy God. Since there is no repentance in their lives, there is no joy and no celebrations in the heavenlies over them.

THE LOST COIN

Our Lord follows that parable with another story to which His audience can also relate. This time there is a woman who lost a coin:

> Or what woman, having ten silver coins, if she loses one coin, does not light a lamp and sweep the house and seek diligently until she finds it? (Luke 15:8)

The first story is about one sheep out of a hundred. This time it is one coin out of ten. We are seeing increased value as the stories progress. When the woman loses this valuable silver coin, just like the shepherd, she searches and searches until she finds it:

> And when she has found it, she calls together her friends and neighbors, saying, "Rejoice with me, for I have found the coin that I had lost." (Luke 15:9)

What happens when this woman finds her lost coin? She celebrates just like the shepherd did. She calls her friends and neighbors to join her in her great joy. That is a picture, Jesus says, of what goes on among the angels of God when one sinner repents:

> Just so, I tell you, there is joy before the angels of God over one sinner who repents. (Luke 15:10)

THE LOST SON

Jesus follows up with another story for His audience made up of the religious leaders, the disciples and the sinners. Again something is lost, but this time what is lost is far more valuable than a sheep or a coin. In this parable, a son is lost:

> And he said, "There was a man who had two sons. And the younger of them said to his father, 'Father, give me the share of property that is coming to me.' And he divided his property between them." (Luke 15:11-12)

As Christ introduces the story, we sense that the son is ambitious, and he feels unsettled in the father's house. He is the younger son. The family is wealthy, and he asks for his share of the inheritance. It does strike us as odd that the father gives a share of the estate while he is still living, but the son is demanding:

> Not many days later, the younger son gathered all he had and took a journey into a far country, and there he squandered his property in reckless living. (Luke 15:13)

The son sets out on his journey with great confidence. At last, he is on his own! No older brother to whom he must answer, no father's expectations to deal with. He is finally free to make the decisions for his own life that are right for him. But he quickly finds himself consumed with the immaturity of his own life and the poor choices that result from his uncontrolled desires:

The Day of the Lord!

> And when he had spent everything, a severe famine arose in that country, and he began to be in need. (Luke 15:14)

What incredibly poor timing! Just as he runs out of money, a famine strikes. He knows, that if it were not for the famine, he would surely be able to get his life together. But now the whole world seems to be against him. Day after day, he seeks work but there is none available. He is hungry and has no place to go:

> So he went and hired himself out to one of the citizens of that country, who sent him into his fields to feed pigs. And he was longing to be fed with the pods that the pigs ate, and no one gave him anything. (Luke 15:15-16)

Finally, the young man is able to find work. It isn't much of a job, and it is so degrading. He is taking care of pigs, those detestable animals that the pagan Gentiles eat! He is in a distant country, so alone and so hungry. He wishes he could eat what the pigs eat. It is then that he comes to his senses:

> But when he came to himself, he said, "How many of my father's hired servants have more than enough bread, but I perish here with hunger!" (Luke 15:17)

How often do we, or people we know, spend time "living with the pigs" before we come to our senses? That is what happens to the young man in Jesus' story. All of a sudden, it dawns on him: his father's hired workers live better than this! They have more than enough to eat. He makes a decision to return home, and he prepares a speech for his father:

> I will arise and go to my father, and I will say to him, "Father, I have sinned against heaven and before you. I am no longer worthy to be called your son. Treat me as one of your hired servants." (Luke 15:18-19)

204

Can you imagine the thought of returning to the father when you are alone and hurting? What hope must fill the heart of this young man! But, in reality, the hope is only that his father will give him a job. He really has no hope that his father will take him back as a son. He knows that he has given up his position as a son and squandered his father's resources.

The young man heads home. He is tired and alone; he is weak and hungry. His own failures and sin humiliate him. He knows that the issues of his wild living at his father's expense will have to be confronted:

> And he arose and came to his father. But while he was still a long way off, his father saw him and felt compassion, and ran and embraced him and kissed him. (Luke 15:20)

As the son, who wanted to go his own way more than he desired a relationship with his father, returns home, he is undoubtedly filled with guilt, fear and shame. But long before he can arrive at home, his father sees him on the road. His father, who must have been watching day after day for his son to return, is not filled with anger as he remembers the independent and rebellious spirit of his son; he is filled with compassion. He does not wait for this wayward and lonely young man to knock on the door, humble himself and ask forgiveness. Instead, he runs to his son and embraces him:

> And the son said to him, "Father, I have sinned against heaven and before you. I am no longer worthy to be called your son." (Luke 15:21)

The lost son is trying to get the words out, to give the prepared speech that he wrote before he left that far away land, but it seems as if the father is hardly listening. He is giving orders to his servants to quickly bring the things that affirm the sonship of his wayward child. He is preparing to carry his son home, just as the shepherd carried the lost sheep home on his shoulders:

> But the father said to his servants, "Bring quickly the best robe, and put it on him, and put a ring on his hand, and shoes on his feet." (Luke 15:22)

The father orders the best robe to place upon his son's shoulders, just as our Father does for us as He clothes us in the righteousness of His own Son. He places the ring on his son's finger, signifying the relationship is restored, just as our Father does in our adoption as His children. Then the father prepares the feast of celebration, just as our Father is preparing the marriage feast for the bride of His Son:

> "And bring the fattened calf and kill it, and let us eat and celebrate. For this my son was dead, and is alive again; he was lost, and is found." And they began to celebrate. (Luke 15:23-24)

The son says to his father, "I am no longer worthy to be called your son." However, in every way the father is affirming the sonship of his child who lost his way and almost lost his life in the process. He is a son, not because his performances earned him that position; he is a son because he has a father. It is the father who restores the son's place in the family. Now there is only one thing left to do. "Let's have a feast and celebrate!"

THE RIGHTEOUS OLDER SON

While all of this is taking place, there is an older son out working in the field. When he returns from the labor that his father entrusted to him, he hears all of the noise and the commotion:

Now his older son was in the field, and as he came and drew near to the house, he heard music and dancing. (Luke 15:25)

As the older son inquires of the servants, he hears for the first time about the return of the wayward son. "The news is so exciting to the father," the servants tell him, "that he is planning this incredible party so we all can celebrate with joy":

> And he called one of the servants and asked what these things meant. And he said to him, "Your brother has come, and your father has killed the fattened calf, because he has received him back safe and sound." (Luke 15:26-27)

The news that is so exciting to the father is not so exciting to the older brother. He is offended and confused. It is not right to celebrate such rebellion and sin. He withdraws from the party and the father:

> But he was angry and refused to go in. His father came out and entreated him, (Luke 15:28)

Now the same father that sought the younger son on the road back from failure and shame seeks the older son who is lost in his anger and pride. This is the heart of a father who searches for sheep, coins and sons that are lost. He does that because his heart seeks reconciliation and redemption. Just as he reconciled his son who was lost in his rebellion, he now seeks to reconcile the son who is lost in his pride:

> but he answered his father, "Look, these many years I have served you, and I never disobeyed your command, yet you never gave me a young goat, that I might celebrate with my friends." (Luke 15:29)

The older son is not easily persuaded to join in the celebrations. In his eyes, this level of joy in response to that level of sin is completely inappropriate. We see now that the older son is not only proud and angry, he is hurt. He reminds his father of his own faithfulness and his hard work. Yet, his father has never even given him a small goat for a dinner with his friends:

> "But when this son of yours came, who has devoured your property with prostitutes, you killed the fattened calf for him!" (Luke 15:30)

We can see the anger in the son's eyes. We can hear the pain in his voice. In all of his faithfulness, he never felt recognition from the father. But now this son who squandered the father's wealth with prostitutes comes home, and there is this big party. It is all so wrong! The father's faithful love remains, and he continues his ministry of reconciliation:

> And he said to him, "Son, you are always with me, and all that is mine is yours. It was fitting to celebrate and be glad, for this your brother was dead, and is alive; he was lost, and is found." (Luke 15:31-32)

The father first affirms the sonship of the older brother. Then he explains the reason for the great celebrations. It is the only fitting response, he says, because they had all thought the younger son had died. Now they learned that he is alive and has returned home. The only way to respond to news like that is to celebrate. The only fitting response to redemption is joy!

The father's ministry of reconciliation does not stop at the restoration of his relationship with his lost son. His focus is now on the relationship between the two brothers. In his great hurt and offense, the older son says to his father, "This son of yours." In response, the father says, "This brother of yours." Just as he took the initiative in healing the relationship with his son, he now takes the initiative in healing the relationship between the two brothers.

Jesus begins the series of parables in this chapter with the Pharisees who are surprised that He would allow sinners to gather around Him. He ends the chapter with the Pharisee who is the older son. Repentance is a powerful theme in the three stories. In the first, there is more rejoicing over one sinner who repents than over ninety-nine who do not need to repent. In the second, there are angels who rejoice over one sinner who repents. In the last, there is one son who needs to repent, and another who has no such need in his own eyes. It is the one who repents who stimulates the incredible celebrations in the father's house.

The second great theme that we see in these three parables is that of joy. There is rejoicing in heaven when one sinner repents. In the presence of God, the angels rejoice over one sinner's repentance. When the prodigal returns, there is an amazing party with feasting, singing and dancing. Heaven is filled with rejoicing and celebrations that reflect our Father's joy over the repentance of those who return to Him. There is one continual party in the heavenlies as the hosts of God join in the Father's delight as He is bringing to Himself those who will be saved.

LET'S HAVE A FEAST AND CELEBRATE!

One of my closest friends and coworkers in the ministry is Gary Olson, pastor of evangelism at our home church. Gary is a serious man. He is serious about his work, his wife, and his family. He is serious about his walk with the Lord. Because it is his nature to take the things of God seriously, Gary faces discouragement from time to time. There are times, however, when the face of my brother lights up with a radiance that is glorious. The joys of family times bring him great delight. The other times that I see his face light up with joy are when he sees people placing their faith in Christ.

Through Gary's ministry, we erected a wooden cross that stands just to the right of the platform in the front of our church. Gary invites his brothers and sisters to place on that cross the names of family members, friends and coworkers who do not know Christ. We pray consistently for those whose names are on that cross, and when a person is converted, we rejoice. Gary's face shines the brightest when he takes a name off that cross and introduces to us a new member of the Body of Christ. Gary knows how to join the party going on in heaven. He knows how to enter into the Father's joy.

In chapter three, "God's Heart for His World," we looked at two motivations for missions and evangelism: the glory of God and the joy of the nations. We are looking at a third here: our own joy as we join in the celebrations of our Father's heart.

IS GOD FRUSTRATED?

There are those who feel that God is angry and frustrated about how things are going here on earth. The lack of church growth in the developed nations, the lack of missionaries, the lack of funding for His work, and the small vision for evangelism among His people must grieve Him deeply. Many see a God who is limited by the disobedience of His people and concerned about whether His will might ever be fulfilled. That is not the God of the Scriptures or the God of the heavenly celebrations.

Surely, God cares about all of these things, but He is very happy with Himself and what He is doing. God is continually filled with joy in the fulfillment of His will. His sovereign power enables Him to do all that He pleases to His own glory, and He is fully confident that every purpose of His heart will be completed.

God is filled with joy at every moment and celebrates each time He transfers a person from the kingdom of this dark world to the Kingdom of His beloved Son. He wants us to share His joy. The more we enter into the celebrations in the heavenlies, the more we will be motivated by that joy to enter into the harvest.

When Jesus taught His disciples the parable of the talents, the master repeated the same affirmation to the good stewards. Our Master, too, is filled with happiness and joy which He desires us to share.

> His master said to him, "Well done, good and faithful servant. You have been faithful over a little; I will set you over much. Enter into the joy of your master." (Matthew 25:23)

DO YOU WANT TO BE BLESSED OR REPAID?

On another occasion, Jesus attends a luncheon at a Pharisee's house. The religious leaders loved to give elaborate feasts, inviting the wealthy, the spiritual and the strong. Of course, they hope to be invited in return. Jesus watches these important and powerful people seeking out the best places at the table:

> He said also to the man who had invited him, "When you give a dinner or a banquet, do not invite your friends or your brothers or your relatives or rich neighbors, lest they also invite you in return and you be repaid." (Luke 14:12)

Jesus confronts His listeners with their consuming desire to be noticed by people and to be repaid. Acceptable spiritual performances before the proper audience are the primary motivation for their lives. They surround themselves with people just like themselves, the elite of their society:

> But when you give a feast, invite the poor, the crippled, the lame, the blind, and you will be blessed, because they cannot repay

you. You will be repaid at the resurrection of the just. (Luke 14:13-14)

Our Lord calls the spiritual leaders of His people to reflect His heart and surround themselves with hurting people, the ones who seldom receive invitations to banquets. If they will do that, they will be blessed. If they are looking to be repaid, they should continue to invite the strong, the wealthy and the beautiful in the eyes of this world. But if they want to be blessed, they should invite the weak and the broken. The wealthy can repay us now, but when we make the poor and the needy our priority, God will repay us at the resurrection:

> When one of those who reclined at table with him heard these things, he said to him, "Blessed is everyone who will eat bread in the kingdom of God!" (Luke 14:15)

Someone in the audience, picking up on Christ's comments concerning the resurrection, begins to talk about the feast in His eternal Kingdom. Jesus responds by telling them another story:

> But he said to him, "A man once gave a great banquet and invited many. And at the time for the banquet he sent his servant to say to those who had been invited, 'Come, for everything is now ready.'" (Luke 14:16-17)

The setting of His parable is a banquet. Perhaps it is a luncheon just like the one they are attending that day. When everything is prepared for the banquet, the host calls his servants to tell those who were invited to come:

> But they all alike began to make excuses. The first said to him, "I have bought a field, and I must go out and see it. Please have me excused." And another said, "I have bought five yoke of oxen, and I go to examine them. Please have me excused." And another

said, "I have married a wife, and therefore I cannot come." (Luke 14:18-20)

Instead of responding to the invitations, those invited begin to make excuses. For one, it is a field that must be seen. For another, it is a new wife who must be cared for. For yet another, the excuse is a new team of oxen:

> So the servant came and reported these things to his master. Then the master of the house became angry and said to his servant, "Go out quickly to the streets and lanes of the city, and bring in the poor and crippled and blind and lame." (Luke 14:21)

I WANT MY HOUSE TO BE FILLED!

How does the host of the banquet respond when his invitations are rejected? He becomes angry! He begins to give his servant new orders. Go out again, he cries, and bring in those who were not invited the first time. Now the command is to focus the invitations on the hurting and the weak:

> And the servant said, "Sir, what you commanded has been done, and still there is room." (Luke 14:22)

The servant of the host explains that they had already invited the poor and the broken, but there still is more room at the banquet. The master commands him to go out again. Before, the command was to go to the streets and the alleys. Now, it is to go to the remote lanes of the country:

> And the master said to the servant, "Go out to the highways and hedges and compel people to come in, that my house may be filled. For I tell you, none of those men who were invited shall taste my banquet." (Luke 14:23-24)

The judgment of the master comes upon those who reject the invitations to his banquet. They are not allowed to even taste of the dinner. But the house is filled with those who are found in the streets and those who live on the country lanes.

Every time I read this parable, my heart is gripped by the Father's desire for His house to be filled and with His heart for hurting people. Our God is preparing a great banquet feast. Attending that banquet will be those from every tribe and tongue and people and nation. His house will be filled with the weak and the broken, the sick and the sinners. The worship will be glorious, it will last forever, and we will be there!

I have been in many meetings, luncheons, and banquets where broken people were seated around the edges of the crowd. Some were in wheelchairs; others were crippled people with crutches and canes; still others needed to carry tanks of oxygen with them for their very survival. The banquet that our Father is planning will not be like that. There will be no broken people seated on the edges around a group made up of the beautiful and the strong. Those who were broken in this world will have been made whole. The beauty that was theirs even in time will now be revealed in its glory. The poor, the crippled, the blind, and the lame are the only ones invited to the banquet in our Father's house, and the invitations to this banquet are entrusted to you and me.

There is one other thing worth noting about the feast that the Father is preparing. The only ones who qualify to deliver the invitations are the poor, the crippled, the blind, and the lame. The strong and the beautiful in the eyes of this world do not qualify to send out the message that "all things are now ready." Only the weak and the broken can be used by the Master to fill His house in preparation for His eternal celebrations!

THE JOY OF THE FATHER'S WILL

One day when Jesus was looking with compassion at the multitudes of hurting people around Him, He said to His disciples:

> Then he said to his disciples, "The harvest is plentiful, but the laborers are few; therefore pray earnestly to the Lord of the harvest to send out laborers into his harvest." (Matthew 9:37-38)

Our Father invites us to join Him for His harvest and for the feast He is preparing. Obedience to His call and the willingness to lay down our lives in the process are necessary if we would follow. The joy we experience along the way and the rejoicing that will be ours in the presence of our Lord and His angels when we are "repaid at the resurrection of the righteous," will move us with our Father's heart of evangelism.

One of the books that God has used to move me to love Him, to know Him and serve Him is Jim Elliot's diary, recorded in his wife Elisabeth's book, *Shadow of the Almighty*. On September 3, 1952, Jim was in Ecuador where he, in a few short years, would give his life for the Auca Indians. On that evening, he wrote:

> Surely life is full in His will and brings promise of good things yet for us here. In spite of my wait since Friday, first for the teacher and then for the plane, the thought kept recurring as I came along the trail, "right on time, right on time-God's time." So with much joy we have arrived at last at my destination decided on in the Will when at Wycliffe in 1950, and my joy is full, full, full. Oh how blind it would have been to reject the leading of those days! How it has changed the course of life for me and added such a host of joys.[17]

---

[17]Elisabeth Elliot, *Shadow of the Almighty: The Life & Testament of Jim Elliot*, (New York: Harper & Brothers, Publishers, 1958), p. 185.

Jim Elliot's joys carried him into the will of the Father and into the incredible harvest God had prepared for him. It is when we enter into the Father's joy that we, too, find the fullness of satisfaction that enables us to serve Him. It is part of His preparation for us to meet the Bridegroom!

GROUP STUDY GUIDE
AND PERSONAL APPLICATION

1. Peter tells us that "God's patience means salvation." Which of your family members, friends and neighbors come to your mind as you read that Scripture?

2. When you think of the "sinners" and the "mutterers" mentioned in Luke 15, which of those do you most identify with? Why?

3. Was there a time when God found you as a lost sheep, put you on His shoulders and carried you home? Describe that experience, and how your heart responded to it.

4. Each of the parables in Luke 15 is a picture of the incredible rejoicing that takes place in heaven over one sinner who repents. What is it that causes this amazing joy? Is each person that valuable, or is something else causing that celebrating to break forth?

5. Do you think that the father of the prodigal responded properly? Wouldn't some discipline or some "tough love" have been more appropriate?

6. Which of the two sons tells the story of your life? Why?

7. Is your life characterized by the joy of the shepherd, the woman, the father and the angels? Why, or why not?

8. Do you see a God who is frustrated with the way things are going in missions and evangelism, or a God who is continually celebrating, and confident in the fulfillment of His will?

9. God desires His house to be filled with the poor, the crippled, the blind and the lame. Do you have enough relationships with these people to participate with God in that process?

REFLECTIONS, COMMITMENTS AND PRAYER

Perhaps as you have studied Luke 15, you are confronted with the fact that the level of joy in your life is far less than what God desires for you to share with Him. You may be hungrier than ever to join the parties taking place in the heavenlies. Ask the Father to lead you into His joy and to fill your heart with the celebrations of heaven as you see people coming to repentance.

Ask God to lay a person on your heart who needs to repent, and have the Shepherd carry them home. Make a commitment to pray every day for an entire year that God would draw that person to Himself.

...be diligent to be found by him without spot or blemish, and at peace.

2 Peter 3:14b

9

Be at Peace with God

Peter has called us to hope, to share God's heart for this world, to holiness and to look forward to Christ's Second Advent. The Apostle Peter comes now to the summary statements of his second letter. Since we are looking forward to all that God promises in The Day of the Lord, he calls us to holiness once again and then to peace:

> Therefore, beloved, since you are waiting for these, be diligent to be found by him without spot or blemish, and at peace. (2 Peter 3:14)

We are found spotless as we place our faith in Christ, receiving Him as our Savior and Lord, and as God clothes us with the righteousness of His Son. We live blameless lives as we pursue righteousness and His Kingdom with all of our hearts. Peter reminds us that the patience of God means salvation for those we love, those for whom we are praying:

> And count the patience of our Lord as salvation, just as our be-
> loved brother Paul also wrote to you according to the wisdom
> given him, (2 Peter 3:15)

Peter gives us insight now into how some of the Apostle Paul's
letters are seen. Peter affirms the consistency of Paul's message
in his letters and then touches on something that many of us can
identify with:

> as he does in all his letters when he speaks in them of these mat-
> ters. There are some things in them that are hard to understand,
> which the ignorant and unstable twist to their own destruction,
> as they do the other Scriptures. (2 Peter 3:16)

We are not the only ones who have had difficulty understanding some of Paul's letters! Peter freely confesses that but warns
about "twisting the Scriptures." What an affirmation we see here
in Peter's statement! It is clear that the apostles know that they
are writing the Scriptures. They are fully aware that the Holy
Spirit is giving them the very Word of God.

HANDLE THE WORD OF GOD CAREFULLY

When Peter talks about those who distort the truth, he actually is
returning to a theme that he begins in his second chapter. He
warns the people about false prophets and false teachers:

> But false prophets also arose among the people, just as there will
> be false teachers among you, who will secretly bring in destruc-
> tive heresies, even denying the Master who bought them, bring-
> ing upon themselves swift destruction. (2 Peter 2:1)

Just as there are those who deliberately forget, there are
those who secretly, purposefully, introduce heresies that destroy
not only themselves but those who hear them. Peter even

equates false teaching with denying God. Such is the serious-
ness of heresy:

> And many will follow their sensuality, and because of them the
> way of truth will be blasphemed. And in their greed they will ex-
> ploit you with false words. Their condemnation from long ago is
> not idle, and their destruction is not asleep. (2 Peter 2:2-3)

Peter lays bare the motive of those who distort the truth. It is
greed. Perhaps greed for financial gain or reputation or greed to
be elevated in the eyes of others is what moves false teachers. It is
without question the desire for self-enhancement. God tells us
what is awaiting them. Condemnation and destruction are prepared for those who distort the Scriptures.

When you know that you are handling the very words of God,
you handle them carefully. Paul talks to the church at Corinth
about these same things. After teaching his brothers and sisters
about not losing heart in the ministry, he talked also about not
falling into the manipulations and deceptions of those who use
the Scriptures shamefully to their own advantage:

> But we have renounced disgraceful, underhanded ways. We re-
> fuse to practice cunning or to tamper with God's word, but by the
> open statement of the truth we would commend ourselves to ev-
> eryone's conscience in the sight of God. (2 Corinthians 4:2)

There is integrity and character in the Word of God, and His
servants must handle the Scriptures with integrity and character as well. If, in ministry, our confidence is in God and the words
that He speaks, if we truly believe that He is able to heal, cleanse,
create life and bring encouragement and hope through His Word,
then we will not manipulate nor distort the Scriptures.

The Day of the Lord!

Do Not Be Carried Away

Paul and Peter placed their hope in the Word of God for their ministries to His Church. Peter warned those who would distort the Word of God that they were preparing themselves for destruction. He describes that destruction in The Day of the Lord. Peter now sets another warning before the people of God.

> You therefore, beloved, knowing this beforehand, take care that you are not carried away with the error of lawless people and lose your own stability. (2 Peter 3:17)

Since there are teachers who are quite willing to distort the Scriptures, manipulating them to say what the false teachers want them to say rather than what God is saying, be on guard. Peter is once again reminding his readers of what they already know, but he warns them about "not being carried away by error." He is concerned that they might "fall away" from their secure position.

Those who submit to false teaching are vulnerable to falling away from the security they find in God and in His Word. We often see brothers and sisters in Christ being carried away by the errors of "lawless men," those who possess neither integrity nor character, and who refuse to submit themselves to the authority of the Scriptures. We, too, must fiercely protect the sheep of God's Church from false teachers.

We also need to receive the warnings of God's Word concerning falling away. There is no question in the Scriptures that a person who has a responsive heart before the Lord is secure in His presence. But we need to be very careful not to give assurance of salvation to a person who is in rebellion against the Lord and pursuing a lifestyle of sin or where we do not see any fruit of the

Holy Spirit in his or her life. Paul confronted the church in Corinth in just that way:

> Examine yourselves, to see whether you are in the faith. Test yourselves. Or do you not realize this about yourselves, that Jesus Christ is in you? —unless indeed you fail to meet the test! (2 Corinthians 13:5)

We do not preach on Scriptures like this often enough in our churches. We do need to be examining ourselves, testing ourselves, asking hard questions of ourselves. We cannot place our hope and confidence in a "decision" that was made some years ago if there is never any evidence or fruit of Christ's life within us. And we are not being helpful to our family members and friends if we allow them to do that either.

MAKE YOUR CALLING AND ELECTION SURE

The Apostle Peter confronts his readers with that same truth in the very beginning of his second letter, which we are studying in this book. After describing the character qualities that reflect God's heart—faith, goodness, knowledge, self-control, perseverance, godliness, brotherly kindness, and love (2 Peter 1:3-7)—in the life of the believer, Peter says:

> For if these qualities are yours and are increasing, they keep you from being ineffective or unfruitful in the knowledge of our Lord Jesus Christ. (2 Peter 1:8)

The life of God expressed through us by means of the Holy Spirit enables us to be fruitful in our walk with the Lord. Peter calls us to possess these qualities in increasing measure. We need to grow continually in Christlikeness in order to be His servants. Peter then sets before us an even stronger warning:

> For whoever lacks these qualities is so nearsighted that he is blind, having forgotten that he was cleansed from his former sins. (2 Peter 1:9)

If you do not possess these character qualities of godliness, Peter says, you are living in blindness and you have forgotten that you are cleansed from your sins in the first place. This, then, is Peter's conclusion for his readers:

> Therefore, brothers, be all the more diligent to make your calling and election sure, for if you practice these qualities you will never fall. For in this way there will be richly provided for you an entrance into the eternal kingdom of our Lord and Savior Jesus Christ. (2 Peter 1:10-11)

If we hunger for God's heart to be built into us and to become conformed to the image of Christ, Peter says, we will be eager and diligent to "make our calling and election sure." How can we do that? Isn't God's call in our lives based only on His sovereign grace and mercy? How can we make His calling sure in our lives? We confirm his call through faith by seeking Him, pursuing Him with a whole heart, and walking in the fruit that He will fulfill in us.

The Apostle Paul exhorted the church at Corinth in the same way as Peter called us to "make our calling and election sure." At the close of his letter, Paul said:

> Examine yourselves, to see whether you are in the faith. Test yourselves. Or do you not realize this about yourselves, that Jesus Christ is in you? —unless indeed you fail to meet the test! (2 Corinthians 13:5)

We need to talk to ourselves and one another like Paul did to the Corinthian church. We need to ask hard questions like Peter did about fruit. Placing our confidence in anything less than the Cross, whether it be a religious experience or the sincerity of our hearts or the performances of good works that seek God's approval, will not produce a sense of peace with God in our hearts. Only a faith firmly focused on the work of Christ at Calvary and His blood poured out for our sins, and the fruit that His life within us produces, will give us that assurance.

Peter comes back to those great truths now as he closes his letter. He warns us to guard ourselves from falling. Be careful of lawless men who have no regard for us or for the Word of God. And then he calls us to grow in God's grace:

> But grow in the grace and knowledge of our Lord and Savior Jesus Christ. To him be the glory both now and to the day of eternity. Amen. (2 Peter 3:18)

Do not be carried away, Peter says, but grow in God's grace. Let the roots of your life sink deeply into His wonderful heart and draw on His great love and power. When we grow in the grace of our Lord and Savior, God puts His glory on display in our lives as we wait for the soon return of Jesus Christ.

BE CONTENT

Peter calls us to be at peace with God while we are awaiting the return of His Son. The writer to the Hebrews teaches us about that very same process of preparation. As he completes his teaching toward the end of chapter twelve, he describes the fear and trembling that characterized the hearts of His people when they assembled before Him at Mount Sinai. He then contrasts that fear with the freedom and confidence that characterizes the hearts of His people today as we stand before Him in His eternal Kingdom. After he tells us that God is preparing time for eternity and that we are receiving a Kingdom which cannot be shaken, he calls us to respond to hurting people with the heart of God:

225

> Let brotherly love continue. Do not neglect to show hospitality to strangers, for thereby some have entertained angels unawares. (Hebrews 13:1-2)

The writer encourages us to continue loving our brothers and sisters. He then sets before us that amazing possibility: sometimes when we think that we are entertaining strangers, we are actually ministering to angels! He calls us to then focus that love of the brethren on those who are in painful circumstances:

> Remember those who are in prison, as though in prison with them, and those who are mistreated, since you also are in the body. (Hebrews 13:3)

Following up his call to remember strangers, the writer focuses our attention now on those who are forgotten, prisoners, and those who are hurting and mistreated. Our Father has a heart for hurting people, and He desires for us to share His heart toward them as well:

> Let marriage be held in honor among all, and let the marriage bed be undefiled, for God will judge the sexually immoral and adulterous. (Hebrews 13:4)

The writer to the Hebrews also talks to us about our marriages. If we are walking in holiness and desiring God's glory, we will honor marriage and our marriage partners. All of the aspects of holiness—being "other" than those around us, keeping pure before the Lord, and being set apart for God's purposes—are reflected in the marriage commitments of those who are preparing to meet the Bridegroom:

> Keep your life free from love of money, and be content with what you have, for he has said, "I will never leave you nor forsake you." (Hebrews 13:5)

What is the next area of contentment to which we are called? It is our finances. This is an incredibly strong exhortation from the writer to the Hebrews: "Keep your lives free from the love of money." How our hearts are vulnerable in this area! There is only one thing that will protect our hearts here and that is contentment. Again and again, the Scriptures tell us what God's will is for us financially. It is contentment. Unless we are content with what we have, we will become enslaved by our cravings for more and consumed by those things we desire:

> So we can confidently say, "The Lord is my helper; I will not fear; what can man do to me?" (Hebrews 13:6)

Why can we be content with what we have? Because God is there and His provisions are sufficient. That is what the writer is teaching us. After he calls us to be content with what we have, he reminds us, "Because God has said 'never will I leave you.'" Now we can be confident that since God is our helper, we have no one to fear.

God is teaching us the secrets of contentment, one of His most precious gifts. When we are content in our marriage, content with whom God has given us as a partner, content with what the Father has entrusted to us financially, and content with His presence in our lives, our hearts are free to serve and to worship Him. This is how God sets us free from the insatiable cravings for more, from the pressures to produce what will glorify us, and from the striving that destroys hearts and relationships.

Some months ago as I was driving to a time of ministry, I began to meditate on God's goodness to me. As I was thinking and praying, I realized how content I am with my wife, Karen, with my sons, with my finances, and with my ministry. This is a great gift from the Lord. It enables a wonderful level of freedom to flow in my heart that empowers me to serve.

When the writer reminds us of God's promised presence, he is telling us that our Father expects that to be enough for us. When we are content in God—in His provisions and in His presence—we are enjoying one of His richest gifts.

This issue was at the very heart of King David's sin. He committed adultery with Bathsheba and then murdered her husband, Uriah. When Nathan the prophet confronted him, he said:

> Thus says the LORD, the God of Israel, "I anointed you king over Israel, and I delivered you out of the hand of Saul. And I gave you your master's house and your master's wives into your arms and gave you the house of Israel and of Judah. And if this were too little, I would add to you as much more." (2 Samuel 12:7b-8)

If we are not content and satisfied in God and in His gracious provisions for us, we will seek to satisfy our souls with whatever our flesh is craving. God is saying to us through the writer to the Hebrews and through the prophet Nathan, "Am I not enough for you? Am I not sufficient to supply your every need?" When He is enough, our hearts are free.

WE HAVE AN ANCHOR

When Peter calls us to "be at peace with Him," it is in the context of being found spotless and blameless before God. There is only one way that we can be pure in His eyes, and that is the sacrifice of His own Son. All of our hope is in the cross of Calvary where, at a point in history, God poured out the blood of Jesus that washed away our sins. Through our faith in Him, we stand holy before a righteous God with our hearts at peace because His wrath was spent on Jesus rather than on us.

The writer to the Hebrews tells us that God swears by Himself (because there is no one greater to swear by—Heb.6:13) concerning His covenant promises toward us. By His promises, we are His children through Abraham. And then he says:

> so that by two unchangeable things, in which it is impossible for God to lie, we who have fled for refuge might have strong encouragement to hold fast to the hope set before us. (Hebrews 6:18)

Those two unchangeable things are God's person and His promises. By His character, it is impossible for God to lie. And His Word is settled forever in heaven. On that secure foundation, we run to take hold of the hope of salvation. It is that hope which fills us with encouragement, even in the midst of our sufferings and a world that is passing away. And what does that hope do for us?

> We have this as a sure and steadfast anchor of the soul, a hope that enters into the inner place behind the curtain, where Jesus has gone as a forerunner on our behalf, having become a high priest forever after the order of Melchizedek. (Hebrews 6:19-20)

Our hope in the unchangeable character of God and His Word provides an anchor for our souls. That anchor is firm and secure; it is not moved when relationships and circumstances change or when the earth is shaken. Why is that anchor so secure? Because it is strongly grounded in God's "holy of holies," behind the curtain that separated us from Him in our sin.

We have talked considerably in our study about afflictions and suffering. We have been honest about the pain that we bear as we take up the cross and follow Jesus. The Christian life is one of great joy and often great disappointment. Truthfully, we face one storm after another as God is preparing us for His heavenly kingdom. What do we do when a great storm strikes the ship of our lives, our marriages, families and ministries? We need to get the anchor down! We need something to hold us fast until the storm has passed. The only place where our anchor can hold is in God and in the places of redemption He provides for us at the cross.

Why is our hope anchored "behind the curtain in the inner sanctuary?" It is because of the nature of our enemy and the way he attacks us. Satan will continually lie to us about God, about ourselves and our relationship with Him. He will try to manipulate us into seeing ourselves through his eyes rather than through the eyes of God. If we see ourselves in light of our past, our feelings or our failures, our faith will be shipwrecked on the rocks of our great enemy's lies. These are some of the greatest storms our faith will ever face. When these storms hit us, we will be vulnerable to doubts and fears, and sometimes we will feel abandoned and alone. The truth of the cross is our only hope in the face of these terrible and frightening storms.

There was a time in history at a place called Calvary where Jesus Himself entered into the Holy of Holies and placed His own blood on the Father's mercy seat for your sin and mine. He completely satisfied the wrath of a holy God against us. The veil of the temple was torn in two (Luke 23:45) and through Jesus' redemption we were brought into relationship with our heavenly Father.

If our hope and security are founded in our religious practices or our sincerity before God or our good life, we have no hope at all. If our hope is grounded in our careers, our investments, or our families, all of these will be shaken. Only in the "inner sanctuary" can we find a place secure enough to anchor our souls. Only behind that curtain can we live at peace with God as we are preparing to meet the Bridegroom.

CHILDREN OF THE LIGHT

The Apostle Paul closed his first letter to the church at Thessalonica with a strong challenge to be prepared for the coming of the Lord. Undoubtedly, they had asked about times and dates, but he turned their hearts toward the realities of The Day of the Lord:

> Now concerning the times and the seasons, brothers, you have no need to have anything written to you. For you yourselves are fully aware that the day of the Lord will come like a thief in the night. (1 Thessalonians 5:1-2)

We do not know why Paul does not feel the need to write to his brothers and sisters in Thessalonica about "times and dates." Perhaps he thinks that it is all irrelevant, or perhaps he takes for granted that they already know all that they need to know. The first thing he sets before them is that The Day of the Lord will come like a thief in the night. When so many least expect Christ to return, when they are least prepared, He will come:

> While people are saying, "There is peace and security," then sudden destruction will come upon them as labor pains come upon a pregnant woman, and they will not escape. (1 Thessalonians 5:3)

For the children of God who have faith in Christ, The Day of the Lord is filled with hope. For unbelievers, that Day is something to dread. When people feel most secure, destruction will come. It will come suddenly, like a woman gripped with labor pains. Even though many will seek to escape, there will be no safety and no place to hide:

> But you are not in darkness, brothers, for that day to surprise you like a thief. (1 Thessalonians 5:4)

We as believers should not be surprised when the Day comes because we do not live in darkness, seeking to hide from God and from one another. It should not come upon us like a thief, since God has taught us to be prepared:

> For you are all children of light, children of the day. We are not of the night or of the darkness. So then let us not sleep, as others do, but let us keep awake and be sober. (1 Thessalonians 5:5-6)

Since we are children of the light rather than of the darkness, we must not live like others. Children of the night sleep in the darkness. We are not like them, Paul says, and so we are not to be found sleeping, but to be aware and disciplined. Living lives of readiness and service is a major aspect of preparing to meet the Bridegroom:

> For those who sleep, sleep at night, and those who get drunk, are drunk at night. But since we belong to the day, let us be sober, having put on the breastplate of faith and love, and for a helmet the hope of salvation. (1 Thessalonians 5:7-8)

Sleeping and drunkenness are characteristics of the night. What are the characteristics of the day? Discipline, faith, love, and hope—those things that express holiness and righteousness are what mark the day. This is the lifestyle we model before one another and the world if we are looking forward to that blessed hope that is our inheritance in Christ Jesus:

> For God has not destined us for wrath, but to obtain salvation through our Lord Jesus Christ, who died for us so that whether we are awake or asleep we might live with him. (1 Thessalonians 5:9-10)

Our Father does not appoint us to suffer the wrath of The Day of the Lord. He calls us to receive the salvation prepared for us since the foundation of the world. The price that is paid for our redemption was the blood of His own Son. It is not only our for-giveness from sin that God seeks in the cross but a relationship of intimacy and fellowship as well.

THE HEART OF GOD

What should be our responses to God's grace to us in The Day of The Lord? How should we live in light of His salvation and mercy? Paul turns now to our relationships with one another:

> Therefore encourage one another and build one another up, just as you are doing. (1 Thessalonians 5:11)

Our relationships ought to be filled with encouragement in light of Christ's soon return, Paul says. We need to be building each other up in the things of God and in the hope He brings. Continue doing that, even as you are doing now:

> We ask you, brothers, to respect those who labor among you and are over you in the Lord and admonish you, and to esteem them very highly in love because of their work. Be at peace among yourselves. (1 Thessalonians 5:12-13)

How do we build up one another? We do that with respect, es-pecially for those whom God places over us. There is a spirit of submission reflected here as well. Our spiritual shepherds, our pastors and elders, are gifts the Father gives to us for protection, teaching and direction. We esteem them and love them because of how they lay down their lives for us. In all of our relationships in God's Church, we pursue peace with one another:

> And we urge you, brothers, admonish the idle, encourage the fainthearted, help the weak, be patient with them all. See that no one repays anyone evil for evil, but always seek to do good to one another and to everyone. (1 Thessalonians 5:14-15)

Paul continues to describe ministries of confrontation, encouragement and mercy. In patience we seek justice and cover it all with an attitude of kindness. Then he brings us to joy, prayer and thankfulness. These are the things that God's will is all about:

> Rejoice always, pray without ceasing, give thanks in all circumstances; for this is the will of God in Christ Jesus for you.
> (1 Thessalonians 5:16-18)

This Scripture is one of the most beautiful descriptions of God's heart that we see anywhere in His Word. These attitudes and relationships reflect who He is and what He is like. Where else in this world would we see such encouragement and the desire to build up one another? What other environment is characterized by respect, peace, help, and patience? Is there any place other than our churches where we find such kindness, joy and thankfulness?

How do we prepare to meet the Bridegroom? It is by giving the heart of God to one another! This is our greatest need among God's people today. We face such pressure and pain every day in this world. Our church needs to be a place where completely different things happen. There we need to bring each other those things that come from God's heart. Our relationships of love become a sanctuary of healing and protection in the midst of an evil world.

We do not train our people well enough that this is what church is all about. We have come to worship insight in today's church to such a degree that our people actually believe that the purpose of their trip to the service is to gain some new insight from the Bible, a "nugget from God's Word" that they can take home with them and ponder. That is why one of the most common things that is said to the pastor as people file past him after the sermon is, "You really gave me something to think about to-day." When was the last time we heard someone say, "I saw something of the beauty of God's heart today, His mercy, forgiveness and grace that I never saw before? It led me to worship Him, and it made me more hungry to be like Him. I want to give myself to people the way He does."

That seldom happens because we have made our minds the center of our Christian experience rather than our hearts. Minds are critically important. Theology is foundational. But in many of our churches we have incredibly expanded minds, while at the same time we struggle with sexual sin, materialism, anger, pride, bitterness and broken relationships just like the rest of the world. Only the glorious heart of God will change us and only touching others with the wonder of His heart will enable them to be healed.

The gift and the ministry of encouragement expressed within the Body of Christ is one of our greatest needs as we are preparing to meet the Bridegroom. The writer to the Hebrews described it this way:

> And let us consider how to stir up one another to love and good works, not neglecting to meet together, as is the habit of some, but encouraging one another, and all the more as you see the Day drawing near. (Hebrews 10:24-25)

DO NOT PUT OUT THE SPIRIT'S FIRE

Paul closes his letter with further exhortations that help us to prepare to meet our Bridegroom:

> Do not quench the Spirit. Do not despise prophecies, but test everything; hold fast what is good. Abstain from every form of evil. (1 Thessalonians 5:19-22)

What a call for the Church of the Lord Jesus today! How we need the Spirit's fire to fall upon us to consume our passions for God's glory, to fill us with His power, and to cause our lives to overflow with His fruit. We desperately need the fire of the Spirit's gifts among us and His presence around us. Many of our churches that once were alive are now dead because they put out the Spirit's fire. We need to welcome prophecies that are tested and rooted in God's Word. We must hate what is evil and cling to what is good:

> Now may the God of peace himself sanctify you completely, and may your whole spirit and soul and body be kept blameless at the coming of our Lord Jesus Christ. He who calls you is faithful; he will surely do it. (1 Thessalonians 5:23-24)

Now Paul brings us again to the hope we have in Christ. The God who brings peace will purify us and set us apart for Himself. He will prepare us for His return when we respond with the heart of a lover to His call in our lives. He will make us entirely His and keep us blameless until the coming of His Son. He is faithful; He will do it!

KEEP YOUR LAMPS BURNING

Jesus tells another parable to His disciples to help them prepare for His return. The story is of ten virgins waiting for the bridegroom. Five are wise, and five are foolish:

> Then the kingdom of heaven will be like ten virgins who took their lamps and went to meet the bridegroom. Five of them were foolish, and five were wise. (Matthew 25:1-2)

What is the difference between the wise and the foolish virgins? It is in their preparation for the coming of the bridegroom:

For when the foolish took their lamps, they took no oil with them, but the wise took flasks of oil with their lamps. As the bridegroom was delayed, they all became drowsy and slept. (Matthew 25:3-5)

The wise virgins take with them the oil needed to keep their lamps burning as they wait for the bridegroom, but those who are foolish take no oil. They wait and wait for the bridegroom, but he takes a lot longer coming for them than they had anticipated:

But at midnight there was a cry, "Here is the bridegroom! Come out to meet him." (Matthew 25:6)

When the virgins least expect the bridegroom to come, he arrives. They are all sleeping, and at midnight, the cry rings out, "The bridegroom is here! It is time to meet him!":

Then all those virgins rose and trimmed their lamps. And the foolish said to the wise, "Give us some of your oil, for our lamps are going out." (Matthew 25:7-8)

All the virgins awaken and prepare to raise the flame in their lamps, but some of them are almost out of oil. They seek help from the virgins who prepared sufficiently but there is not enough oil for them all:

But the wise answered, saying, "Since there will not be enough for us and for you, go rather to the dealers and buy for yourselves." (Matthew 25:9)

The virgins who are prepared are not selfish. They know that there is so little time, and they have to be ready. The only possibility for the unprepared virgins is to quickly go out and find some oil to purchase:

And while they were going to buy, the bridegroom came, and those who were ready went in with him to the marriage feast, and the door was shut. (Matthew 25:10)

The bridegroom comes while the unprepared virgins are out searching for oil for their lamps. The virgins who are prepared go in to the banquet but the door is closed against those who are not ready:

> Afterward the other virgins came also, saying, "Lord, lord, open to us." But he answered, "Truly, I say to you, I do not know you." (Matthew 25:11-12)

Later, perhaps when they are able to find the oil that they need for their lamps, the unwise virgins return to the house where the banquet is being held. They begin to cry out for the door to be opened, but the bridegroom refuses. He does not know them. They do not share in his banquet:

> Watch therefore, for you know neither the day nor the hour. (Matthew 25:13)

WHAT KIND OF BRIDE IS THIS?

When we look at the parable of our Lord, we ask hard questions about the readiness of His bride. In many ways, we do not appear to be watching with our lamps burning. We seem to have allowed our lamps to run out of oil while we have fallen asleep.

As I travel around the world, I am deeply troubled when I see the condition of the bride. In some places, we see brokenness and division. In other places, we see selfishness and pride. Still other parts of the Body struggle with false teaching and other parts with materialism. When we visit churches in one country, we might be confronted with a lack of zeal for missions, in other places there is no hunger for holiness. What kind of bride is this?

The Apostle John tells us one reason why the Church is struggling in these very areas that I have mentioned. The Lord Jesus says in His letter to the church at Ephesus:

To the angel of the church in Ephesus write: "The words of him who holds the seven stars in his right hand, who walks among the seven golden lampstands. 'I know your works, your toil and your patient endurance, and how you cannot bear with those who are evil, but have tested those who call themselves apostles and are not, and found them to be false. I know you are enduring patiently and bearing up for my name's sake, and you have not grown weary.'" (Revelation 2:1-3)

This is strong affirmation coming from the lips of our Lord for the church in Ephesus. They work hard, and they endure. They love the truth. There is incredible, lasting fruit in their ministry. They sound just like a very successful church in suburban America! One thing, however, is missing:

But I have this against you, that you have abandoned the love you had at first. Remember therefore from where you have fallen; repent, and do the works you did at first. If not, I will come to you and remove your lampstand from its place, unless you repent. Yet this you have: you hate the works of the Nicolaitans, which I also hate. (Revelation 2:4-6)

In the midst of all of their hard work and endurance, the church at Ephesus had forsaken their first love. They lost the passion for Christ that was once theirs. Without that passionate love for their Lord, nothing of their other accomplishments matters! It is the passions of our hearts that drive us in life and ministry, and it is those same passions that our Lover most desires.

My heart breaks as I look at the state of our churches in the developed nations. Sexual sin is rampant. Materialism reigns. Anger and bitterness consume relationships. The divorce rate mirrors the rest of the world. People come into our churches and make commitments. They hear the Word of God preached week after week, and they join in the worship. But it seems that the first time the Scriptures conflict with the desires of this world in their hearts or the temptations to sin pull at their passions or the elders call them to submission, they are gone.

We preach the Scriptures well from our pulpits today. We teach Christianity well. We sing about it well. We celebrate it well. We just don't do it very well. Why? Because we have given the passions of our hearts away to lesser loves. We, like the church at Ephesus, must rekindle our first love. How do we do that? It begins with seeing ourselves through the eyes of God and repenting. Turning away from the lesser loves that consume us, we can ask God to stir within us once again the passion that held our hearts fast to our Lover when we first saw the beauty of His face and the purity of His desire for us. As we then walk openly before Him—hungering for intimacy once again and desiring to please Him—that love and passion will be fanned into a flame which will consume us.

I must admit that I have fought cynicism as I look at the Church today. Many times when I see who we are and what we are like, I am vulnerable to losing heart. What keeps me from giving up in ministry is the knowledge that Jesus promises to build His Church, and that the God whom we serve is confident and resting securely in the fulfillment of His will. He is very happy with the way things are going in the heavenlies. Our God is celebrating His victories every moment and rejoicing continually in the advancement of His Kingdom.

What kind of bride is the Body of Christ? The Scriptures tell us clearly. She is holy, pure and glorious! The bride is radiant in Her beauty, with not even one blemish! If we would be of any value in the Kingdom, we will learn to see the Church through the eyes of the Bridegroom:

Husbands, love your wives, as Christ loved the church and gave himself up for her, that he might sanctify her, having cleansed her by the washing of water with the word, so that he might present the church to himself in splendor, without spot or wrinkle or any such thing, that she might be holy and without blemish. (Ephesians 5:25-27)

Is it significant that this is the same church, the church at Ephesus, that we see in the book of Revelation? This is what the Church looks like after it has been transformed by the passionate, purifying love of the Bridegroom. This is a bride worth loving and worthy of our every means of serving. Jesus gave His life for the bride that Paul describes to the church at Ephesus. When we see her through the eyes of the Bridegroom, we will lay down our lives, too, in order that her beauty will shine forth until the Bridegroom comes.

IF JESUS WOULD RETURN TOMORROW...

If we knew that Jesus would return tomorrow, what difference would that make in our lives? Would we allow bitterness and a lack of forgiveness to divide families if we knew that Jesus would come tomorrow? Would we allow consumerism to steal away resources from the building of God's Church around the world? Would anger and pride still split churches? Would we allow our lusts to drive us rather than a passionate love for God? If we knew that Jesus would return tomorrow, would marriage partners still contemplate leaving one another and abandoning their children? Sadly, the answer to these questions is, "Yes!"

Why would we continue in our selfishness and sin if we knew Jesus would return tomorrow? Because there is no such thing as tomorrow! Tomorrow is one of Satan's most effective lies. It never comes; tomorrow is only an illusion. That is why the Scriptures say:

> Today, if you hear his voice, do not harden your hearts. (Hebrews 4:7b)

The only time that God gives us to respond to Him is today. If we will not walk before him in holiness and obedience today, we will not tomorrow. If not now, when? Many of God's people have seen their lives, their families and incredibly glorious ministries stolen away in a thousand tomorrows that have never come. If God speaks to your heart through these Scriptures that we have studied, come to Him now with a whole heart, and seek Him while He may be found by you:

> Seek the LORD while he may be found; call upon him while he is near; (Isaiah 55:6)

I WANT TO MARRY YOU

A part of my family heritage is Jewish. In the Jewish tradition, if a father seeks a young man for his daughter in marriage, he might approach a "matchmaker" to arrange a meeting with the young man's family. If there is a positive response, the two fathers might negotiate a "bride price," or perhaps that price might be negotiated by the young man himself. When the price is settled upon, it is up to the young man to approach the potential bride.

The bridegroom comes with a cup of wine in his hands. He holds out the wine to the young woman whom he desires to marry. As he holds out the cup, he is saying, "Will you marry me?" If the young woman takes the cup, she is saying, "Yes, I will marry you!"

Our Father set His affections upon us even from eternity, and He arranged a marriage for you and me. He negotiated the price, and He paid the price. That price was the life of His Son. The Son of God comes now to you and me with a cup in His hands. That cup is filled with the wine of His love, and He is holding it out to us. He is saying, "Will you marry me? I want you to be my wife." He is inviting us to reach out and take that cup. Our Lord desires us to say, "I will marry you. I want you to be my husband."

When we take that cup, a lifetime of preparation begins. The Bridegroom will make us ready by the power of His life within us. Our Lord desires a pure and beautiful bride, one who is His alone, who shares His love and His heart. He paid the highest price to purchase His bride and to prepare her to be glorious in His eyes.

Our calling now is to prepare our hearts and our lives and to be ready when He comes to take us to His bridal chamber. He wants to see the beauty of His glory reflected in our eyes. Jesus desires for us to meet Him with the heart of a lover. Every purpose of time and every longing of our hearts will be fulfilled in The Day of the Lord when the Father sends the Son to meet His Bride!

GROUP STUDY GUIDE
AND PERSONAL APPLICATION

1. Do you see yourself as spotless and blameless before the Lord? Why, or why not?

2. Have you had experiences where you, or those around you, were "carried away by error?" How did that experience end?

3. How do you respond to the teaching on "examining yourself to see if you are in the faith," and "making your calling and election sure?" Have you spent much time in that process? What resulted from it?

4. What is the level of your contentment in God and what He has provided for you? Where do you most need to grow in these areas?

5. The heart of God is beautifully described in 1 Thessalonians 5:11-16. Do you see that heart modeled and shared within the fellowship of believers in your church? Where do you see the greatest need for growth concerning these things?

6. When you study the parable of the ten virgins in Matthew 25, which group of five do you most identify with? Why?

7. Have you struggled with me as you look at the state of the Church today? How have you responded to that? Do you think that you see the Church through the eyes of God?

8. Where in your life have you struggled with the "tomorrows?" What would God have you do?

9. As you visualize the Lord Jesus holding His cup out to you, what are the things that you think of concerning your preparation for His coming for you to be His bride?

REFLECTIONS, COMMITMENTS AND PRAYER

Make your first response to these studies a heart of worship before the Lord for choosing you to be His Bride. Ask God to fill your heart with a sense of awe and wonder in His presence for His great and faithful love toward you. Pray that He would show you how to prepare for His coming in order for you to be all that He has called you to be. Reach out, take that cup which Jesus holds in His hand, and commit yourself to His process of preparation for you to be the Bride fit for His wedding banquet!

Scripture Index

The Day of the Lord!

The Day of the Lord!

1 JOHN

2:15-16	168
2:17	168

REVELATION

1:1	42
1:1-2	43
1:3	44
2:1-3	239
2:4-6	239
5:6	160
5:7-8	161
5:9-10	81
5:9-10	161
5:11-12	161
5:13	162
5:14	162
19:11	154
19:12	154
19:13	154
19:14	155
19:15	155
19:16	155
20:4-5	153
21:1	156
21:2	156
21:3	156
21:4	157
21:5	157
21:6-7	157
21:8	158
22:1-2	159
22:3-4	159
22:5	160
22:7	44
22:20	45

Leadership Resources
International

If you have been encouraged by this book, you might consider using it in a small group or class in your church. You might also consider inviting Bill to teach the Bible conference "Preparing to Meet the Bridegroom," which is based on this book, in your church.

Our desire is to magnify God in the eyes of His people so that they may stand in awe, wonder and worship before Him, and be transformed in His presence. We do this as we bring the encouragement of the Scriptures to churches, pastors and missions. The largest aspect of our work is encouraging and equipping pastors in the developing world who often have little formal training for the ministry. These ministries take place throughout Latin America, China, Burma, Russia and Africa. We invite your church to partner with us in one of these training times.

For more information about our conferences or materials, contact:

Leadership Resources
12575 South Ridgeland Avenue
Palos Heights, IL 60463
(800) 980–2226
www.leadershipresources.org